Ancient Indian Magic and Folklore

Ancient Indian Magic and Folklore

An Introduction

MARGARET STUTLEY

GREAT EASTERN
BOULDER 1980

First Published in 1980
by Great Eastern Book Company
P.O. Box 271
Boulder, Colorado 80306

Printed in Great Britain

Library of Congress Cataloging in Publication Data

Stutley, Margaret, 1917-

Ancient Indian magic and folklore.

Bibliography: P.
Includes index.
1. Magic – India. 2. Charms. I. Title.
BF 1622.I5S78 133.4'4 79-13211

ISBN 0 87773 712 6

To my husband,
who has helped and encouraged me so much

Contents

Illustrations

Preface

This brief introductory study of ancient Indian magic and folklore is based mainly on the *Atharvaveda* (compiled c. 1400 BC).

During man's existence he finds himself confronted by phenomena, often mysterious, which he strives to explain by classifying the relationships between living beings and the external world into two main classes – the ordinary and the mysterious or magical. A feeling of unease occurs when something fails to fit into his preconceived categories, which may account for the animosity and fear that exist between particular cultural and racial groups. Correct classification can enable man to increase his knowledge, but faulty classification, arising from his lack of knowledge of natural law, leads to strange by-ways from whence arises the belief in the power of deities, demons, angels, witches, animals and sorcerers, and in the efficacy of curses, spells and the Evil Eye. But any classification – by seeming to allay uncertainty and tension – promotes a feeling of mastery of the individual's situation. Man's greatest fear is the common unsolved problem of death, which has given rise to much speculation in the past concerning immortality, and which still continues.

Magic and cult are a means of making man's life less fear-ridden, more hopeful and secure by the expectation that in times of trouble, transcendental powers will protect him if the correct ritual, appropriate offerings, oblations, sacrifices, mantras and prayers are carried out.

Essentially magic and cult are the same, since all rites are basically magical, any difference being that of the method used to influence or propitiate the unknown powers. But these rites show the continuity and the changes in man's beliefs over the centuries, as well as linking the present with the relevant past.

Abbreviations

AOS	American Oriental Series, New Haven, USA
AV.	*Atharvaveda*
Bṛhadd.	*Bṛhaddevatā*
BSOAS	*Bulletin of the School of Oriental and African Studies*, London
ERE	*Encyclopaedia of Religion and Ethics*, ed. James Hastings, 13 vols, Edinburgh, 1908–21
HOS	Harvard Oriental Series
JA	*Journal Asiatique*
JAOS	*Journal of the American Oriental Society*
JRAS	*Journal of the Royal Asiatic Society*
Kauś.	*Kauśika Sūtra*
ME	Middle English
RAS	Royal Asiatic Society, London
RV.	*Ṛgveda*
SBE	Sacred Books of the East
ŚBr.	*Śatapatha Brāhmaṇa*
Suś. Saṁ.	*Suśruta Saṁhitā*
SV.	*Sāmaveda*
Tait. Br.	*Taittirīya Brāhmaṇa*
Tait. Saṁ.	*Taittirīya Saṁhitā*
YV.	*Yajurveda*

Introduction

The family and tribal groups of north-west India during the fourth millennium BC relied largely on magical formulas for the fulfilment of their aspirations, and hence their belief that magic was synonymous with transcendent power. These people were of diverse ethnic origin: from the black proto-Australoid indigenes to the Mediterranean migrant groups (including Dravidians), 'who came to India with a fairly high level of civilization. As contrasted with the proto-Australoid . . . whose culture was mainly . . . based on primitive agriculture, these Dravidian-speaking . . . peoples . . . in India were responsible for cities and a city culture – for a real *civilization* in the true sense of the word. . . .'[1]

About 2000–1500 BC successive groups of Aryans from the Caspian area entered Iran and north-west India. Their white skins, blue eyes, fair hair, and language pattern distinguished them from the brown-complexioned Dravidians and contrasted strongly with the dark-skinned indigenes. Their advent was of particular significance as it coincided with the transition from a relatively primitive period to what historians call the Vedic Age. During this period hereditary priestly (brahmanical) families established themselves as custodians of sacred lore and were thus able to introduce changes, including the formation of a corpus of sacred compositions (*saṁhitās*), the first and most important being the *Ṛgveda*. Though it reflects the influence of ancient folk-beliefs and includes a number of magical formulas, it is the main source of information about early Indian social, political, religious and linguistic development. None the less, traditional beliefs in magical formulas persisted, and spells, charms, incantations, mantras and the use of amulets continued to be recognized as instrumental in securing prosperity, good health, longevity, success in love, offspring, the defeat of enemies and the averting of calamity. Hence about 1400 BC an attempt was made to collect these formulas. This collection was ascribed to the legendary fire-priest or priest-magician Atharvan, who in later mythology was said to be the son of Brahmā. From Brahmā he received the *brahmavidyā*, the foundation of all knowledge, which was then successively passed on to Aṅgir, Bhāradvāja Satyavāha, and Aṅgiras (*Muṇḍaka Upaniṣad*, I.1f.). Another smaller collection was added shortly after and ascribed to the priest-magicians Bhṛgu and Aṅgiras.

Over the centuries attempts were made to have this combined collection of magical formulas added to the sacred corpus (that is the three Vedas – *Ṛgveda*, *Yajurveda* and *Sāmaveda*), but without success. Not until a number of additions, chiefly from the *Ṛgveda*, had been made was it added to the original Veda. In accordance with custom, ritual texts and other works – such as Upaniṣads – were added over the centuries to each of the *saṁhitās*, and to the *Atharvaveda*, a particular manual of ritual – the *Kauśika Sūtra* – was added. This *sūtra* throws light on some of the obscure passages of the *Atharvaveda*. It is also invaluable for the information it gives of indigenous folk-customs, beliefs and practices. The contents resemble those of the household books (*Gṛhya sūtras*), and comprise various rites including those to placate Nirṛti, the goddess of misfortune and bad luck in general; healing remedies; spells and imprecations; marriage rites; and expiations to avert the evil effects of bad omens and portents; the gaining of wealth, health, and the capacity to overcome rivals and enemies. The *Atharvaveda-pariśiṣṭas* also deal with similar subjects.

The two extant recensions of the *Atharvaveda*[2] are traditionally associated with the Śaunaka and Paippalada priestly schools, the former being used in this study. To Śaunaka also is attributed the *Ṛgvidhāna* (a magico-religious manual of great importance for the history of religions) which was initially 'seen' by the ancient *ṛṣis* who knew the mantras for which Śaunaka drew up the rites. It specifies the Ṛgvedic *sūktas* (songs of praise, the so-called 'hymns') associated with various rites. The *Bṛhaddevatā*, also attributed to Śaunaka, names the deities connected with each of the *RV. sūktas* and includes a number of myths and legends. It is essential to know the name of each deity addressed in the mantras, since no religious merit can be obtained solely from the performance of rites, nor would the rites be efficacious.

The Śaunaka recension of the *AV.* comprises 730 prayers or songs of praise, charms, spells, etc. subdivided into twenty books, but parts of it are separated from each other by centuries. Chronological difficulties occur with most Indian texts and the *AV.* is no exception, but Winternitz considers that the atharvanic magical poetry is as old as, or 'older than, the sacrificial poetry of the *Ṛgveda* . . . numerous [parts] . . . date back into the same dim prehistoric times as the oldest songs of the *Ṛgveda*.'[3]

The association of fire-priests with the Vedic fire-cult is indicated by the *RV.* passage (X.21,5) which states that Agni, the god of fire, owed his origin to Atharvan, and in *RV.* (X.62,5) the Āṅgirasas are said to have been born of Agni. The *Nirukta* (3,17) further connects the Āṅgirasas with fire by stating that Aṅgiras was born from live coals (*aṅgara*). In the later *Avesta* the general term for priests is *āthravan*, which formerly was thought to be derived from the Avestan term for fire '*atar*', but this is now rejected on philological grounds.[4]

The fire-god Agni was the chief demon-expeller among the

gods, and hence one of his epithets was Aṅgiratama (having the luminous quality of the Āṅgirasas). Furthermore, the mythical seer, Āṅgirasa Bṛhaspati, was regarded as the priestly adviser (*purohita*) and magician of the gods. His name indicates that he was the master (*pati*) of the innermost spiritual force '*bṛh, brahman*, which works magic through communion with the divine'.[5] He was also the 'master of witchcraft and healing, since through him the curative plants release man from pain and grief' (*RV*. X.97, 15–19). But the divine plants, like the powers and forces of the cosmos, remain indifferent to man's desires and needs until correctly 'stimulated' by established magico-religious ritual. These powers in themselves are neutral, and can be utilized for good or bad ends according to the intention of the performer of the rite, since there is no essential difference between cult and magic with which man seeks to influence the transcendental world. Thus *Atharvavedapariśiṣṭa*, 26, describes the properties of logs used as fuel in various ceremonies and states that they may be employed for good or evil purposes. Similarly, some of the Biblical Psalms may be used for exorcism,[6] cursing, killing enemies, or for blessings, offspring and so on.

The belief that the fire-priests alone were capable of producing fire probably gave rise to the myth that the use of the fire-sticks (*araṇis*) was a magical process and a divine gift – a notion which greatly enhanced the priests' status and authority. The fire itself was greatly venerated and subsequently personified and deified as the god Agni.[7] The altar-fire was not only sacred but regarded as the centre of the world (*RV*. I.143,3) and the family hearth was called 'a treasure, established among mankind for mankind' (*RV*. I. 58,6).

The *Atharvaveda* has been much 'brahmanized' over the centuries, making it difficult to distinguish the charms and spells of the Indian indigenes from those of the Vedic priests, since many of the ancient magical songs no longer retain their original form. Nor is it possible to state precisely what were the functions that distinguished the Atharvans and Āṅgirasas. Both practised sorcery, but it appears that the Āṅgirasas undertook the more dangerous magical practices,[8] their most important function being to protect the sacrifice from demonic attacks by means of the atharvanic magical formulas, since regular and correct sacrificial performances were essential to sustain the world.

The appointment of a *purohita* to assist the ruler was regarded as essential to preserve good relations between priests and the secular power; he was also required to perform the necessary magico-religious rites to overthrow enemies – both human and demonic. The later law books insist that a king's *purohita* must be schooled in atharvanic lore (*Yājñavalkya Dharmaśāstra*, I.312). According to the *Laws of Manu* (XI.33), the mantras of the *Atharvaveda* are weapons that a priest may legitimately use to destroy his enemies, but in the same work the practice of sorcery by means of sacrifices is forbidden, and also the common atharvanic practice of magic by means of roots (*mūla-kriyā*). On the whole the law books and the Brāhmaṇas disapprove of many atharvanic practices and lay down severe penalties for those who perform prohibited rites; neither do they approve of fortune-telling, astrology and the practice of medicine which was regarded as an impure profession, probably because of the polluting effect of contact with corpses.

The Atharvans were particularly adept exorcists and employed the names of the gods (because of their inherent power) for this purpose.[9] The ritual utterance of sacred names to 'bind' demons was also common in Sumeria, Babylonia, Assyria and ancient Egypt. Sometimes the Atharvans employed the philosophical concept of non-being (*a-sat*), which was personified and regarded as an entity capable of destroying sorcery and witchcraft. This is similar to the use of the term *ajanani* (non-birth) used in cursing: 'May he cease to exist!' and to the modern British slang expression, 'Drop dead!'

Although the names of many Vedic divinities were later included in the *Atharvaveda*, much of their 'individuality' was lost, their names being employed ritually to increase the efficacy of rites. However, most of the atharvanic demons' names do not appear in any other texts – an indication that they belong to an early non-Aryan stratum of beliefs.

The *Atharvaveda* is generally recognized as the basis of Hindu medicine (*āyurveda*), traditionally expounded in two ancient texts, the *Caraka* and *Súsruta Saṁhitās*, which present the first attempt to distinguish 'between magico-religious treatment and rational therapeutics based upon *yukti*, i.e., rational connection of observed facts'.[10]

The *Atharvaveda* is invaluable for the study of the institutional history of early India, and its folklore records the popular beliefs and customs of the people over many centuries. Some of these beliefs spread to the Far East and to Europe.

ONE

Medical charms

Vedic medicine was a combination of magico-religious rites, intuition, an extensive knowledge of nature-lore and herbal remedies, and recognition of the effects of climate. The priest–physicians were also sometimes able to recognize a relationship between phenomena not obviously related.

> An intriguing characteristic of ancient medicine is that it incorporated most aspects of knowledge. Ancient physicians were concerned with the physiological effects of music, astronomical events, and religious beliefs, just as they were interested in anatomical structure, surgical techniques or the activities of drugs. Through the catholicism of their attitude, ancient medicine became the mother of the sciences, the inspiration of humanism, and the integrating force of culture.[1]

The texts of the *Ṛgveda* and *Atharvaveda* are the two earliest Indo-Aryan sources of Indian medicine, some of which stem from the proto-historical period and thus constitute an invaluable source of archaic beliefs. But the earliest extant medical 'handbook' (now in the University Museum, Philadelphia) is a Sumerian tablet in cuneiform script which records the favourite remedies of an anonymous Sumerian physician who lived at the end of the third millennium BC. This tablet lay buried in the ruins of Nippur for over four thousand years until excavated by an American archaeological expedition. From it we learn that the Sumerian *materia medica* consisted of particular plants (those with odoriferous properties being especially prized), and of animals and minerals. It is evident that Sumerian pharmacology had made considerable progress even at that early date, as potassium nitrate is mentioned – a substance which could not have been obtained without some knowledge of chemistry. Probably the Sumerians collected nitrogenous waste products from drains and removed for purification whatever crystalline formation was found. The difficulty of separating the components was probably overcome

> by the method of fractional crystallization. In India and Egypt there is still current the ancient procedure of mixing lime or old mortar with decomposing nitrogenous organic matter to form calcium nitrate, which is then lixiviated and boiled with wood ash containing potassium carbonate to yield niter on evaporation of the filtrate.[2]

The Vedic *materia medica* consisted initially of herbal and vegetative substances, minerals not being added until about the beginning of the present era. The curative effects of some of these medicaments were later corroborated by medical science, but others cannot now be identified. A number of Vedic prescriptions bear a general resemblance to the traditional pharmacopoeia of the West before the advent of modern pharmacology and experimental chemistry. The complexity of many of the Vedic prescriptions stems from the conservative basis of all archaic medicine which insisted that no part of a prescription, once approved, should ever be omitted lest it prove to be the ingredient essential to the cure, but there was no limit to the addition of other ingredients. Diet was also carefully studied – both in sickness and in health – and adapted to prevailing climatic conditions, but at the same time great reliance was placed on the use of amulets, talismans, spells, philtres, and mantras, the last believed to contain, in the form of magical sound, the essential energy of the divinity invoked. The use of incantations or mantras in conjunction with remedial rites was common throughout the ancient world and many parts of the modern world; in Europe today some patients recite a Pater

Noster or Ave Maria, or make the sign of the Cross when taking medicine.

Like animals, early man had instincts which helped him to minimize the effects of disease. He also realized that many mysterious forces (mysterious, because outside the range of his understanding and control) affected his health and well-being – a realization which enabled magical practices to play an essential part in his attitude and beliefs concerning the causation and control of disease. To early man magic, religion and medicine were one. Disease was thought of as a spirit external to man which now and then afflicted him (*RV.* X.97,11 and 13).

The laying on of hands for healing was practised in Ṛgvedic times and probably much earlier. The hands are called the two 'chasers of disease' which stroke the patient 'with a gentle touch' (X.137,7; see also X.60,12).

Much of Hindu classical medicine developed from the herbal lore and magical beliefs of the Vedas, and like the medical beliefs of ancient and medieval Europe up to the eighteenth century, was based on the concept of particular elementary substances or humours (*dhātu*; *doṣa*). The three humours – wind, bile and phlegm – when evenly balanced with blood as a fourth *doṣa* ensured a healthy body (*Suś. Saṁ.* I.21). The *doṣas* were identified with the three universal forces, wind, sun and moon respectively. When the *doṣas* are in equilibrium they support the body firmly and it is then likened to a three-pillared building: thus the body is sometimes called the 'three-pillared one'. The three primary *doṣas* are also equated with the three *guṇas* (universal 'qualities') of the Sāṁkhya system.[3]

The atharvanics attributed most diseases to demons, as did their counterparts in other ancient cultures. Thus many diseases have the same names as the demons believed to have caused them, but some of the names appear only in the *AV.* Demons also inflicted bad luck, poverty, misfortune, and death. When the name of the disease-demon is known to the priest it passes into his power, because in magic a verbal statement is an efficient symbolical imitation of an act.

The *RV.* (VII.50,4) refers to a disease demoness called Śimidā; a later medical work (*Suś. Saṁ.* I.43) states that many illnesses are 'due to the malignant influences of conjured up she-devils'; others to the adverse influences exerted by particular stars or planets (I.141). Planets were believed directly to affect such illnesses as smallpox, scarlet fever and measles, as well as the growth of plants, and the general affairs of mankind.

Demons gain access to a person's body when one is eating or yawning. The Hebrews associated the Devil with the open mouth according to one of their proverbs: 'Open not thy mouth to Satan!' Moslems place the backs of their left hands against their mouths when yawning and say: 'I seek refuge with Allah from Satan, the accursed.' *Tait. Saṁ.* 2.5,3, states that one who yawns should say: 'Skill and intelligence remain in me . . . ,' but the Evenk shamans of Siberia yawn deliberately to receive into themselves the spirits they wish to evoke.[4]

Gods also may send disease to those who have offended them. Varuṇa is especially associated with the sending of dropsy, because of his connexion with the waters. He also binds liars in his noose but subsequently, when belief in transmigration was accepted, disease was attributed to 'sins' committed in former lives.[5] He binds the liar with seven by seven nooses, or with a hundred of them. Similarly in Babylonia the priest 'binds' demons with holy names, thus holding them 'spellbound'. The priests also regarded sickness as a punishment for having neglected the gods who had created man specifically to serve them. Illness too could be the result of neglecting some duty by the individual or by his parents or clan. In Europe infants suffering from congenital syphilis are sometimes regarded as the innocent victims of their parents' sins. This retributive concept of suffering dominates the Old Testament; the ancient Greeks believed that disease (especially insanity) was caused by the rage of departed generations, thus only by expiatory rites could a cure be ensured.

Some diseases were attributed to hostile sorcery, witchcraft, the effects of curses, the baneful effects of the Evil Eye, all of which might be counteracted by spells, and by healing herbs and plants. The latter appeared 'three ages earlier than the gods', and are called 'mothers' and 'goddesses'. They also bestow success and wealth on their worshippers, according to *RV.* X.97, which is ascribed to a mythical author Bhiṣaj Ātharvaṇa, the Vedic prototype of the doctor (*bhiṣaj*) magician (*ātharvaṇa*), the founder and embodiment of the magic art of healing. The disease-spirits quickly disappear when they see the plants whose king is Soma, the moon-god. Because of the moon-god's close association with plant growth the moon (in which ambrosia (*amṛta*) is stored) is called Oṣadhipati (Lord of herbs), a title also applied to physicians. A curious myth relates that the plants 'communed together' and decided to save from death any man whom a priest undertook to cure.

Fever[6] is called *takman* in the *AV.* but *jvara* in Indian classical medicine and usually refers to malarial fever, a disease particularly prevalent in the hot, damp climate of the Indian river valleys, where it is often accompanied by jaundice, the dreaded 'yellow disease', whose cure required complex charms and incantations. Initially *takman* was probably a fire-demon[7] who became associated with the high temperature occasioned by fever. Takman is said to have been born when Agni, in the form of lightning, struck the terrestrial waters (*AV.* I.25); the *Ṛgveda* refers to Agni having hidden in the plants and waters. 'The seeming paradox of a fiery substance residing in water presents no difficulty if we keep in mind that the waters symbolize the infinite possibilities of life and fertility and also the source of "immortality".'[8]

A spell initially intended to appease the heat of anger

(*manyu*) was also used to dispel fever, heat being common to both (*AV.* VI.42).

The Vedic personification of illnesses and of various emotions, guilt and so forth, is a ritual method enabling man to draw closer to the powers responsible for such afflictions and to cope with them. Classical medicine uses the same method but to a lesser extent. It usually treats the main constituents of the human body as physical entities, though occasionally it resorts 'to the irrational forms of suggestive treatment through magic as an indispensable supplement to rational procedures'.[9] In some post-Vedic compositions fever is personified as a deformed, three-headed demon called Triśiras, representing the three stages of fever – heat, cold, and sweating. The personified Jvara (Fever) is said to be devoted to Śiva one of whose aspects is Kāla Bhairava, the personified power of time in which the animate and inanimate world is inevitably destroyed. According to the *Suś. Saṁ.* (III.211) fever is always present at the time of death when it is manifested as the fiery breath of Rudra (Śiva) the destroyer of all beings.

According to a story in the *Mahābhārata* the personification of fever was born from a drop of sweat which emerged from Śiva's forehead when he became enraged because he had not been invited to attend Dakṣa's sacrifice. When personified Fever appeared as a short, hairy, dark man, with glowing red eyes and tawny beard. His mouth was huge and gaping, and his clothes were red.

To cure fever the ritual (*Kauś.* 26,25) prescribes the recitation of *AV.* I.25 whilst the priest heats an axe, and then dips it in water which is poured over the patient. As it flows over his body it carries away the fever, water being a magically potent purifying agent whether used alone or with other ingredients. The Sumerians, Assyrians and Babylonians regarded it as the source of all existence. An Assyrian spell for good health reads: 'May all that is evil . . . [in the body] of . . . [be carried off] with the water of his body and the washings of his hands, may the river carry it downstream.'[10] The emanation of the great god Ea remains eternally in water and thus by water he could always be invoked. Similarly in Hinduism the waters are regarded as a 'primary materialization of Viṣṇu's *māyā*-energy',[11] and thus a visible manifestation of the divine essence. The Greeks used running water ritually to wash away evil, but when pollution was excessive water from several springs was employed; to purify a murderer it was necessary to draw upon fourteen different springs. Thus the Greeks, like the Indians, regarded ritual pollution, guilt and murder as entities which had intruded or attached themselves to the individual but which could be 'washed off'. The dispersing qualities of water are also referred to in a Hittite myth: 'the water of a pitcher cannot flow backward', and in 2 Sam. 14:14: 'For we must needs die, and are as water spilt on the ground which cannot be gathered up again.' In the *First Gospel of the Infancy of Jesus Christ* the child Jesus kills a boy who had destroyed a fish-pool he had made. As the water ran out Jesus said: 'In like manner as this water . . . vanished, so shall thy life vanish; and presently the boy died.'[12]

Another remedy for fever was the *kuṣṭha* plant (*Costus speciosus* or *arabicus*), the 'strongest of plants', the 'effacer of *takman*' (*AV.* V.4). The Atharvanics regarded it as second only to the sacred *soma* plant. Like the *soma* it grew on the Himālaya, but originated in the third heaven under the divine *aśvattha* tree where Yama (the ruler and judge of the dead) dwells with the other gods (*RV.* X.135,1). The divine *kuṣṭha* was brought down from the celestial sphere in a golden ship with golden tackle. The epithets *viśvabheṣaja* 'cure-all', and *viśvadhāvīrya* 'potent at all times' are applied to it. Its association with the gods made it an especially efficacious remedy; it was also used in a love-charm (VI.102,2) and thus was probably a fragrant plant. Curiously enough the *kuṣṭha* is also the name – or probably a euphemism – for leprosy;[13] the *kuṣṭha* is called 'the heavenly rescuing god' and is invoked to cure fever, and to drive away witches. This plant has three names, the other two being *naghāmāra* (deathless) and *naghāriṣa* (harmless); its 'mother's' name is *jīvāla* (quickening), and its 'father's' *jīvanta* (long-lived) – such notions all increasing its supposed efficacy and power. It was a common atharvanic practice to give 'parentages' to curative plants, an idea stemming from the belief in the inherent power of names.

Both Babylonian and Indian charms sometimes invoked a large number of deities and deified objects (*AV*. V.22) – because the greater the number of divine names, the greater the potency of the spell.

The *kuṣṭha* plant is called 'thou of power' (*vīrya*), and is commanded by the priest to impel the fever downwards to the earth where it will harmlessly disperse, but it is also necessary to placate the fever itself when expelled from the patient. Sometimes the priest sends it away to neighbouring enemy tribes, or to remote or inferior tribes, called Mahāvṛṣas, Mūjavants, Balhikas, Gandhāris, etc. (*AV*. V.22). Possibly fever was thought to have originated in the regions of these tribes and hence it should be returned to them, or possibly the names are based on puns. The *Tait. Saṁ*. (I.8,61) states that Mūjavant is a synonym for a distant region, to which Rudra and his dreaded bow are entreated to depart; the *RV*. (X.34,1) refers to a place (or mountain) called Mūjavān where the *soma* plant grows. Yāska (*Nirukta*, 9,8) considers it to be the name of a mountain so-called because the sacred *muñja* grass grows on it. It has been suggested that the Iranian land called Mužā on the Indo-Iranian borders is identical with the Sanskrit Mūjavant.[14] A similar modern African practice of sending evil in general or sickness in particular away from the country has been recorded. The spirit responsible 'is symbolically removed from one part of the country to another and finally right out of its borders'.[15]

As fever alternates between spells of cold and delirious heat, accompanied by trembling, delirium and coughing, the ritual (*Kauś*. 29.18,19) instructs the priest to give the patient a drink of gruel containing roasted grain, the dregs of which are poured over the patient's head from a copper vessel and into a fire lighted from a forest fire. Dregs, or the remains of sacrificial food (and also objects used ritually), are especially potent and increase the supernatural power associated with the rite, as is indicated by the importance accorded to the 'remainder' (*ucchiṣṭa*) of a sacrifice, which *inter alia* represents the principle of continuity. The roasted grain and red copper vessel both represent heat and therefore fever; the forest fire is preferred because it is caused naturally, that is, spontaneously, or by lightning which occurs in the rainy season when fever and related diseases are most prevalent. A curious statement is contained in the *Ṛgvidhāna* (II.10,4) that 'by offering red fragrant oleanders one will cause fever'. A Babylonian tablet referring to fever declares that its tongue strikes man like lightning, and results in sickness, headache and heart-disease.[16] The Assyrians personified fever which was said to remain invisibly by man.

Intermittent fever is commanded to enter a frog (*AV.* VII.116); or fever can be cooled by the cold moistness of a frog. The ritual (*Kauś.* 32,17) prescribes that the priest should tie blue and red threads round the forelegs of a striped frog which is then tied on to the patient's couch; the patient is sprinkled with water and as it runs down his body the fever is washed off on to the frog. As blue and red are the colours of hostile witchcraft, the demoness Kṛtyā, who personifies sorcery, is also associated with these colours (*RV.* X.85,28). Sorcery is also performed in a blue and red vessel, and blue and red threads are 'laid out against enemies' (*AV.* IV.17,4; VIII.9,24).

An old Bohemian charm against fever prescribes that a green frog, caught in the early morning dew on the day before St George's day, should be sewn into a bag and hung on the neck of the patient who is kept in ignorance of its contents. He recites the Lord's Prayer nine times before sunrise on nine successive days. On the ninth day he prays on his way to the river into which the bag is thrown; he then returns home still praying and without looking back.

Parts of some charms against injury are really battle-charms such as *AV.* I.2, although they may contain other passages pertaining to medical matters. Some diseases are inflicted by the rain-god Parjanya, whose arrows (representing the disease which strikes the patient) Indra is invoked to divert. But rain itself is likened to a shower of arrows and is called 'Parjanya's semen' (*parjanya-retasa iṣ vai*), because it fertilizes the *muñja* reeds from which arrows are made (*RV.* VI.75,15). To avert injury or disease a *muñja*-grass amulet is tied to the patient and he drinks water mixed with earth from an ant-hill. Finally, the patient is smeared with ghee and the priest blows on the afflicted area (*Kauś.* 25,6–9). In *RV.* X.137 and *AV.* IV.13, the wind is invoked to blow away physical infirmity and disease and to 'blow hither healing medicine'. Ant-hills are regarded as living entities and thus are classed with auspicious plants and other growing things; ants (*upajīhvikā*) themselves are consequently regarded as beneficent insects, possessing the god-given power to reveal the presence of healing water. Monier-Williams (*Sanskrit – English Dictionary*) states that one of the three forms of the term for ant, namely, *upajīkā*, may have been the name of a water-deity, which would explain their connexion with healing water.

To cure constipation, earth from a mole-hill is sometimes prescribed because moles are accustomed to moving along dark narrow passages. There is also an etymological connexion, one of the names or epithets of the mole being *ākhukarīṣa* – a compound of *ākhu* 'mole' and *karīṣa* 'excrement'.

For sufferers from constipation and the inability to pass water a reed is used as a catheter (*AV.*I.3). The rain-god Parjanya is called the father of the reed through which the contents of the bladder will quickly flow out. The ritual (*Kauś.* 25,10–19) prescribes that an amulet consisting of a substance conducive to micturition be attached to the patient, who is then given a potion consisting of the juice of a *pūtīka* plant[17] mixed with earth from a mole-hill. He is given an enema and taken for a ride in a vehicle; an arrow is also shot into the air, and the bladder probed. In addition, twenty-one barley-grains in water are poured into a milk pail, an axe placed behind the patient and the liquid poured over the affected part. The patient then drinks a concoction made from *āla* (a creeper or weed found in grainfields), lotus root, and *ula* (musk).[18]

AV. I.12 refers to the 'Seizer' (*grāhi*) who grips the patient's joints and causes a burning sensation in every limb. This is probably rheumatism or arthritis. To cure this affliction the patient should drink a mixture of fat, honey, ghee and sesame oil, after which he dons a turban of *muñja*-grass,[19] and walks away carrying in his left hand a sieve containing parched grain (representing the dehydrating effect of a high temperature), which he scatters with his left hand; in his right he carries a bowstring and axe, so symbolically preventing his pursuit by the demonic forces now exorcized from his body. When he reaches the place where the disease 'seized' him, he puts down the sieve, turban and bowstring and returns home. The discarding of the turban and other objects are symbolic acts designed to draw out the disease from the patient's body and to transfer it to these objects. The use of a headband for the magic transference of disease was also used in Sumeria and ancient Greece. A Sumerian spell to drive away headache reads: 'Take the hair of a virgin kid, let a wise woman spin it on the right side . . . Bind twice seven knots . . . and bind the head of the sick man . . . and cast the Water of the Incantation over him, that the headache may ascend to heaven . . . [or] like . . . water poured out it may go down into the earth.'[20] A mutilated Assyrian tablet also gives part of a charm to remove headaches. It prescribes the collection of a bundle of twigs, water from the confluence of two streams and the binding of the sufferer's head; at eventide the material is cut off and thrown away, whereupon the headache disappears.

The rite against rheumatism continues with the patient putting ghee up his nose, whilst the priest supports his head with a bamboo staff having five knots. The staff in many cultures is a magical conductor of potency, and is the stock-in-trade of both ancient and modern magicians. The ancient Egyptians used rods to perform magical feats, as did Aaron and Moses who 'was learned in all the wisdom of the Egyptians' (Acts 7:22). Moses turned a living serpent into a stick (Exod. 7:10ff.); struck the rock-face and a spring gushed forth. When Aaron struck the waters with his rod they became blood; he struck the earth and it turned into lice. In Greek mythology Rhea struck a mountain to procure water in which to bathe the infant Zeus. Similar examples can be adduced from Canaanite, Hebrew, Greek, African and Christian folklore.

The atharvanic staff has five knots, representing the five seasons of the year which denote totality, and implies that the patient will remain well in the future. Thus the staff transmits to him its total healing power; in other contexts the staff focuses and transmits its possessor's special power to whatever object or person he wishes to influence, either for beneficent or maleficent purposes. The present-day shamans of the Samoyed groups, namely the Enets, Nenets and Selkups, use staffs with five protuberances for the treatment of the sick and when conducting the spirits of the dead to the next world.[21]

Disease-transference was also practised by the Greeks. When the Thessalian Pandarus, who had unsightly marks on his forehead, went to the temple of Asclepius, his head was bound up and he was told to remove the bandage on leaving and dedicate it as an offering to the temple. Pandarus did so and the marks disappeared. In gratitude for the cure he gave Echedorus, a fellow-sufferer attending the temple, some money for an offering to Asclepius, but Echedorus kept it.

When it was time for the removal of his bandage he found that his own marks remained and in addition those of Pandarus![22]

To cure heart-disease and jaundice (*AV.* I.22; *Kauś.* 26, 14ff.) the 'yellowness' (being a symptom of jaundice) and heart-burn are commanded to go up to the sun, a more compatible abode for them. The patient is 'enclosed' in the 'colour of a red bull', probably a red bull-hide or red robe, red representing blood and, by extension, life, strength and vigour. The ancient Greeks, like the Indians, believed that particular objects – like wool, animal-skins or eggs – could absorb harmful and polluting substances. The Red One (*Rohiṇī*), the deity of red cows, also protects the patient and gives him vigour. His jaundice is transferred to parrots, *hāridravas* (yellow wagtails), and other yellow birds, as yellow itself was believed to be the actual manifestation of the demon of the disease, resident in the patient's body, thus it was necessary to transfer it to another living creature. The patient is given water, mixed with the hair of a red bull to drink, the hair absorbing the pollution. More water is poured on to the back of a bull, some of which is drunk by the patient who thereby absorbs the strength of the animal. The patient sits on a stretched bull-hide previously steeped in cow's milk and anointed with dregs of ghee which had been previously offered to the gods. The dregs or residue (*ucchiṣṭa*) of the sacred food or oblation thus shared by the divinities is 'consecrated through the sacramental act of the sacrifice . . . [and] believed to have been transubstantiated into the divine fare of the celestials; it shares the virtues of *soma* and *amṛta* . . . on which the immortals live', and thus it imparts to the patient the power to overcome death.[23] The patient is given milk and a kind of porridge made of *haridrā* (turmeric), after which the priest daubs him from head to foot with the remainder of the yellow coating representing the jaundice. Then he is placed on a couch to the foot of which three yellow birds are tied by their left legs. The coating of porridge is then washed off, the yellowish water running over the birds to whom the jaundice is now transferred. An amulet consisting of a number of hairs from the chest of a red bull glued together with lac and covered with gold is worn by the patient, and the sun is invoked to transfer heart-disease and 'yellowness' to parrots and starlings.

The Babylonians believed that when yellow plants are found in rivers, jaundice will occur in the region where they come to rest.[24] According to Pliny, jaundice could be transferred by merely looking at a starling, whereupon the bird would die. The transference of disease was also customary in many countries including Sumeria, Egypt, Africa and Europe. In ancient Greece plague was transferred to crows by the command: 'Go to the crows'; in Sumeria, disease was transferred to the 'white kid of the god Tammuz', its heart having been removed and placed in the patient's hand, and its carcass laid close by. When the necessary incantations had been recited the disease was assumed to have been transferred to the carcass, which was then thrown out of the house. Sometimes a pig was substituted for the patient. This may have been the intention behind the New Testament story of the Gadarene swine when Jesus caused the devils possessing two men to enter the herd which then rushed headlong to their deaths. An ancient Egyptian cure for migraine was to rub the aching side of the head with a fried fish – the pain then being transferred to the fish.

> This conception may be at the root of the original use of remedies. The word *pharmakon*, whence pharmacy is derived, meant in Greek not only medicament, poison, or magical procedure, but also that which is slain to expiate the crimes of a city, like the scapegoat of Biblical times . . . In other words, it meant 'what carries off disease'.[25]

Siberian shamans also sometimes transfer disease from a sick man to the body of a sacrificed reindeer. Among the West African Ewe people, sickness is swept away with small brooms after its ritual transference to fowls; in the Nias Islands dolls are substituted for the patients and the diseases transferred to them. (A number of such dolls can be seen in the Wellcome Historical Medical Museum, London.) Birdlike dolls are used on the island of Timor-haut in cases of epilepsy, believed to be caused by the intrusion of a bird-shaped spirit. In Wales, as late as the nineteenth century, cocks or hens were taken by sick people to the parish church of Llandegla, and the well of St Tecla near by was circumambulated three times. A woman patient carried a hen in a basket; a man, a cock. An offering of four pence (4*d.*) was made to the well. The patients then returned to the church and circumambulated it thrice whilst reciting the Lord's Prayer, after which they slept in the church. The next day a piece of silver was placed in the poor box, and the cock or hen left in the church, the diseases having been transferred to the birds. The custom of sleeping in church derives from the ancient method of incubation, or temple-sleep, a practice common to the ancient Egyptians, Greeks and others. An old English country cure for thrush prescribed that a live frog be held with its head in the patient's mouth. As it inhaled it drew out the disease from the patient. As late as 1860, a girl of eighteen suffering from tuberculosis was advised by her doctor to marry so that by disseminating the disease among her offspring she would thereby alleviate her own illness. Similar advice was also given to a relative of Somerset Maugham's in the nineteenth century.

A charm against bleeding from wounds, and that caused by disordered menses, mentions a thousand veins in the body (*AV.* I.17). For staunching blood, dust and sand were sprinkled on the wound (*Kauś.* 26,10), but more likely pads filled only with sand were used. The American-Indians controlled bleeding by packing the wound tightly with hot sand, or with wads of eagle down.[26] When Autolycus was wounded in the leg his companions skilfully bandaged his wound and by means of a charm (*epaoidē*) staunched the flow of blood (*Odyssey*, XIX.457). The Greek verb *deô*, 'bind' or 'tie' and 'the Latin *ligare*, frequently designate the act of enchanting by tying or binding'.[27]

Leprosy was a disease common among Eastern peoples, and in India was attributed to a malevolent spirit called *dūṣi*, the 'Spoiler'.[28] According to the Mosaic Law, leprosy is a divine punishment for any violation of morals or ritual. Thus King Uzziah, who was guilty of a ritual transgression, became leprous and until his death lived in a lazar house 'for he was cut off from the house of the Lord' (2 Chr. 26:16–21). The *AV.* (I.23) refers to the white spots of the disease, and thus it was known as *śvetakuṣṭha* (white leprosy). As the spots showed up clearly on dark skins, 'sympathetic magic' necessitated the use of a 'dark' plant as a remedy, or possibly one that blooms only at night, i.e. 'night-born'; its function being to cover up the spots and finally to make them 'fly away'. The identity of the plant is not known, but the commentator considers it to be the *haridrā* (*Curcuma longa,* from whose powdered root turmeric is produced); or it may be the indigo (*nīli*) plant. According to the *AV.* (I.24) the 'dark' plant is the gall of an eagle. An Āsurī[29] (a female Asura) is said to have discovered the remedy for leprosy. The Asuras were usually regarded as demonic and hostile in the teaching of the Vedas, and the name was also applied to the indigenes, whose superior knowledge of the country and guerrilla tactics greatly troubled the Aryan settlers. The Asuras' knowledge of herbal lore was thought by the Aryans to be of divine origin, since they had remedies for snake venom and for serious diseases, and also knew where to find healing water as did ants, thus ants were called the 'daughters of the Asuras'.

For relief from various diseases and wounds, mountain spring water was advocated (*AV.* II.3) and said to be the 'receptacle of a hundred remedies'.

AV. II.8 is a prayer for a cure of a now unknown disease called *kṣetriya* (lit. 'of the field'); some Indologists suggest that it was an inherited disease, others that it was consumption, scrofula or syphilis. But its name suggests that it was a disease contracted in the field, or associated with the womb, as *kṣetra* means both 'field' and 'womb'. The two stars called the 'Unfasteners' are urged to unfasten all the fetters or bonds of the illness, and to make bewitchers fade away at dawn, when by sympathetic magic the disease itself is expected to disappear. According to the ritual (*Kauś*. 26,43; 27,2ff.), an amulet consisting of a clod of earth and some earth from an ant-hill sewn up in the skin of an animal is bound on to the patient. Homage is paid to the plough (*lāṅgala*) and to the poles and yokes. Whitney points out that the Commentary equates *lāṅgala* with *vṛṣabhayuktasīra* 'homage to the specified parts of the plough', or to their divinities. The patient is placed under an ox-drawn plough and then doused; homage is paid to the demon called 'sunken-eyed'. He is then placed in an empty house (*śunyaśālā*), and then into a hole containing housegrass (*śālatṛṇa*) where he is again doused and his mouth rinsed. The house should not only be empty and dilapidated, but also have round windows. The importance of the round windows is paralleled by the magical powers attributed to the holed stones of India and Europe. Many Indian dolmens have a hole in the front slab, perhaps initially intended for offerings to the dead. If an injured arm or leg was placed in the hole a cure was certain. In Europe, up to the beginning of this century, the Crick, or Creeping Stone, at Madron (Cornwall) cured lumbago and other pains if the patient crawled through it nine times against the sun; the Mên-an-Tol, another Cornish holed stone, cured sick children who were passed through it; on Coll (Hebrides) consumptives crawled through a particular holed stone and left food offerings on it. Small holed stones were hung in stables to protect horses against witchcraft, or the stones were hung in bedrooms to prevent the owners having nightmares. Some countrymen still carry small stones in their pockets as good luck charms.

The atharvanic ritual continues with the priest placing the patient's head under a plough harnessed to cattle, and pouring water over his head; the patient is then placed in a ditch (perhaps to limit the spread of the pollution), given water to drink, and finally rinsed down with water, signifying that the disease has been washed off on to the field (*kṣetra*) from which it had supposedly come.

The curative effects of passing between or through particular objects is reflected in the story of Atri's daughter Apālā who suffered from a serious skin disease. Despite the affliction Indra fell in love with her, and she begged him to make her 'fair-skinned'. He agreed and passed her thrice through or between the body of a cart and the yoke, whereupon her first skin was cast off and became a porcupine (*śalyaka*), the next an alligator (*godhā*), and the last a chameleon (*kṛkalāsa*), after which she became fair-skinned (*Bṛhadd.* 6,99ff.; see also *RV.* VIII.80,7). This recalls the curious passage in the *Chāndogya Upaniṣad* (4.1,8), where a man called Raikva was found scratching himself under a cart.

The deciduous horn (*viṣāṇā*) of the gazelle or antelope (*hariṇa*) was another remedy for *kṣetriya* disease. The shedding of horns so different from the permanent horns of domestic cattle, was regarded as uncanny and hence the horns themselves were thought to possess magical powers. The horn is also identified with the *yoni* (*Tait. Saṁ.* VI.1.3,7). In popular belief powdered and burnt antelope horn drives away mosquitoes and scorpions. The southern United States Negroes confine spirits in antelope horn; the American Hopi Indians regard the antelope as a medicine animal. The atharvanics implored the horn to 'unfasten' the *kṣetriya* in the heart, and the two stars – the 'Unfasteners' – to release the fetters of illness.

That worms (*kṛmi*) of various kinds caused disease was a widespread belief in ancient times and still persists in some parts of the world. A Babylonian poem states that toothache originated when the god of justice offered the worm ripe figs and apricots for food, but this failed to satisfy him; he begged to be lifted up from the mud and placed among men's teeth that he might feed on the roots of their jaws. The god agreed but added that 'henceforth and for ever more the mighty hand of Ea shall be against you to crush you.'[30] A similar belief is found in the Homeric 'Hymn to Demeter', and also among the Chinese, the Malays, the Yorubas of Africa and the present-day Marsh Arabs of Iraq. Bone abscesses, osteomyelitis and Pott's disease are called 'souss' (worms) in colloquial Arabic. In the ancient Egyptian Papyrus Anastase (IV.13,6–7) caries were attributed to a worm *fnt*.[31]

Several atharvanic charms are intended for the destruction of worms. In one, Indra is invoked to bruise them with his great mill-stone, and hence the priest makes an offering of *khalva* grains mashed up by a mill-stone. The ritual (*Kauś.* 27,14ff.) prescribes that worms be mixed with ghee, and wound from right to left along the shaft of a black-spotted arrow which is then smashed. The broken arrow is laid on a fire, and the priest, facing south, throws dust over the patient with his left hand. The patient 'grinds' up the dust and places wood on the fire, so symbolically burning up the worms in his body. Particular worms, called *algaṇḍus*, are crushed by an incantation or words of power; and the remainder destroyed by song, that is, a sung spell. A later medical work (*Caraka* III.7) stipulates that worms should be removed by cleansing; next by attacking and 'smashing' (*vighāta*) the matter from which they originated, then by 'appeasing' it (*saṁśamana*), and finally by the elimination of the cause (*nidāna*).

Both the rising sun (*Āditya*) and the setting sun are called upon to smite the four-eyed, whitish, variegated worms (*AV.* II.32.) (Some of the Old Teutonic charms also mention variously coloured worms.) The atharvanics use the same charms against worms as those formerly employed by the ancient *ṛṣis* such as Atri, Kaṇva and Jamadagni. It was also customary to invoke the ancient seers, whose very names lent greater magical efficacy to rites.[32] By means of the same incantation recited by the *ṛṣi* Agastya when he thought he had been poisoned, the priest 'mashes up' the worms (*RV.* I.191). The same spell was also an antidote to the poison of reptiles, insects, scorpions as well as to all vegetal and man-made poisons.

Sarasvatī, the river-goddess, is sometimes invoked to 'grind up' the worms living in the eyes, nostrils and teeth, because she is associated with the curative waters and is also the wife of the creator-god Brahmā, also associated with healing and who is often depicted holding a jar of medicine or salve.

To expel *yakṣma* (possibly a general term for disease), the ritual (*Kauś.* 27,27) uses *AV.* II.33, for the cure of all diseases (*sarvabhaiṣajyam*). This rite was probably used when the disease could not be diagnosed. The *Vājasaneyi Saṁhitā* (XII.97) mentions a hundred kinds of *yakṣma*, and the *Tait. Saṁ.* (II.3,5) refers to consumption as the 'king's disease' (*rāja-yakṣma*), so-called because when the Moon (King Soma) waned, he was its first victim. The utterance of *RV.* X.161 is said to destroy *rāja-yakṣma* (*Bṛhadd.* 8,64).

To cure impotence and restore virility the tree *kapitthaka* (*Feronia elephantum*)[33] is used (*AV.* IV.4). It is called the 'penis-erecting' plant, and was the remedy used by the Gandharva (who is associated with sexual power) to restore the virility of the god Varuṇa. Indra also was closely associated with virility, usually as its bestower, but sometimes as its destroyer, when he emasculated the drought-demon Vṛtra (*RV.* I.32,7). As the bestower of virility, Indra was invoked to endow suppliants with the combined energies (*śuṣma*) of bulls, men, plants, stags, mules, rams and particularly horses, the last being an ancient symbol of virility as signified by their name *vājin* (meaning strength and potency, a term possibly derived from the hypothetical root *vaj* 'to be strong'). This is confirmed by the *aśvamedha* (horse sacrifice) ritual which contains much esoteric sexual symbolism. Thus in classical Indian medicine the term *vājīkaraṇa* 'turning into a stallion' denotes an increase of virility.

For the restoration of virility the plants *ucchuṣmā* and

parivyādha are dug up with an iron instrument. Two decoctions are made from them and poured into milk, and a drawn bow is placed on the lap of the patient, who then drinks the mixture (*Kauś.* 40. 14ff.). The iron instrument may have been a ploughshare – which has long had sexual connotations; the milk represents semen, and the drawn bow the tautness of the erect penis, which is also referred to in *AV.* VI.101. The Commentary states that an amulet of *arka* wood (*Calotropis gigantea*) is the remedy used in this context, but the Bower Manuscript (c. fifth century AD) substitutes pomegranate rind and mustard oil.

An *arka*-wood amulet is also prescribed in *AV.* VI.72, which refers to the black snake (a phallic symbol) which extends itself at will and assumes wondrous forms by means of the Asura's magic (*māyā*), the amulet being besought to do the same for the patient's penis and to make it like that of the elephant, ass and horse. Elsewhere an amulet, fashioned from the skin of a black antelope, is fastened with hairs from the animal's tail to a man desiring virility (*Kauś.* 40,17); but a spell to destroy virility is also included in the *AV.* (VIII.90).

The use of poisoned arrows in Vedic warfare necessitated charms to counteract their ill effects (*AV.* IV.6; *Kauś.* 28,1ff.). The poison is charmed away from all parts of the arrow, as also from the mountain where the poisonous plant grows, and by extension from the weapons of the enemy. Similarly those who gather the poisonous plant, as well as the plant itself, are rendered harmless. The patient should recite the above charm in a low voice and make obeisance to Taksaka, the chief of serpents; while doing so he sips water and is also sprinkled with it. The same procedure may be carried out with water containing a ground-up branch of the *kṛmuka* tree from which the bow (*kārmuka*) is made. The patient is sprinkled with water warmed by placing in it an old heated garment or a piece of heated antelope hide, or heated straw from an old broom – all worthless objects, thus indicating that the poison has been exchanged for other worthless objects (see also *AV.* IV.7,6). A mixed drink is placed in a water-vessel smeared with the dregs of ghee and stirred with two poison-tipped arrows, the points of which are held upwards during the stirring, indicating the flight of the poison upwards from the patient. Lumps of earth are broken into the mixture which is drunk by the patient until he vomits; then he is given ghee mixed with yellow curcuma to drink. Sometimes a minor divinity called Varaṇāvatī is called upon to ward off (*vārayātai*) poison with river-water (*vār*) (*AV.* IV.7).

Varuṇa gave spells to the priests to dissolve snake-venom (*AV.* V.13), and hence a priest's spell counteracts the snake's own poison and commands the venom to return to the reptile and kill it. (Various coloured snakes are mentioned and some are named – Kirātan, Timātan, Āligī, etc.) An eagle (*suparṇa*) was said to be the first creature to consume poison without being adversely affected.[34] An 'eared hedgehog' (porcupine) which came down from the mountains and made the poison harmless is also referred to. To limit the effect of the poison the priest circumambulates the patient to the left, the inauspicious direction, and fastens a bunch of grass to a tuft of his hair. He drives out the poison whilst reciting *AV.* VII.88: 'Go away, thou art an enemy . . . '. The bite is then rubbed with grass which is thrown on the snake responsible for it, or if the reptile has escaped, the grass is thrown on the place where the patient was attacked, thus transferring the poison to the grass. The patient is sprinkled with water heated by burning reeds from old thatch, mixed with grains of sesame. A bowstring is then fastened on him, and he is given a drink of water mixed with earth from a beehive, and another containing the excrement of a porcupine. Finally beeswax is applied to purify him. Beeswax and honey were believed to dispel demons, to rejuvenate and to purify; bee and ant-stings were thought to cure paralysis.[35] During the rite a gourd is tied to the patient's navel to catch any remains of the poison. A similar intention is apparent in the Babylonian magician's method of exorcizing a demon by forcing it into a clay image fastened to the victim. Then the image is removed and broken, thus destroying the demon.

The poison of insects and venom of reptiles, especially black and cross-lined snakes, adders and scorpions, are dispelled by a sweet (*madhu*) plant, said to be the madhukā – a name applied to various trees and plants (*AV.* VII.56). In Europe it was believed that even seeing a snake could result in much misfortune, to avoid which it was necessary to make the sign of the Cross in a circle on the ground and recite the first two lines of Psalm 68: 'Let God arise, let his enemies be scattered; let them also that hate him flee before him.'

Another charm against snake-venom involved Pedu's white serpent-killing horse called Paidva (belonging to Pedu) (*AV.* X.4). Pedu was a royal *ṛṣi* and a devotee of the twin Aśvins who had given him the powerful white horse previously presented to them by Indra (*RV.* I.116,6; 117,9). The White One (the horse) was commanded to crush the snakes with both fore and hind hoofs. The horse, neighing loudly, dived into the waters, and on emerging announced that the fiery poison of the serpents was now as harmless as water-logged wood. Paidva was besought to go before travellers to remove all snakes on the path. A young Kirāta girl is said to have dug up the antidote on the mountains with a golden shovel. The antidote itself was personified as a girl called Taudī who, like the horse Paidva, prepared a 'poison-free path' for others to follow.

The *RV.* (I.118,9) describes the white horse as triumphant, serpent-slaying, invincible in war and impervious to arrows – the winner of a thousand treasures. The horse represents the sun which moves across the sky like a magnificent white horse. In many cultures solar gods are connected with the horse. Sūrya's chariot was drawn by one or seven horses; the solar Viṣṇu had the horse Uccaiḥśravas; and when the Āṅgirasas performed a sacrifice for the Ādityas (sun-gods) their 'gift' (*dakṣiṇā*) was a white horse (*Aitareya Brāhmaṇa* VI.34; *ŚBr.* III.5.1,13). The Greek Helios had a horse-drawn chariot; Odin, the eight-legged horse called Sleipnir; and the Celtic solar god Lugh, the horse Manaan. In Christian mythology Christ will appear as the sun of righteousness mounted on a white horse (Rev. 19:11); Viṣṇu's future *avatāra* (incarnation) Kalki will appear also as a white horse, or in the form of a warrior mounted on a white horse.

The connexion of the horse with snake poisoning is elaborated in the ritual attached to *AV.* X.4, in which an insect called *paidva* (a substitute for the mythical horse) is ground up, and given to the patient who puts the powder up his right nostril with his right thumb. The priest rubs him down from top to toe, the usual method of driving out poison and disease. The bite is then heated with a torch which is thrown on to the snake, or on the place where the attack occurred, thus symbolically returning the poison to its source. The Boulia aboriginals of Australia cure snake-bite by the medicine-man going to the place where the attack occurred and digging out the snake which he pelts with stones. When it is nearly dead he returns with it to the camp where he pulls its skin back halfway and then drowns it.[36]

Dhanvantari, the divine physician of the gods, is regarded as the embodiment of Hindu classical medicine, but Zimmer considers he is 'an inheritance from aboriginal Indian antiquity'[37] which may account for his omission from the Vedic pantheon. Although Dhanvantari made repeated attempts to neutralize snake-venom he was finally compelled to admit defeat, which necessitated his propitiation of the goddess Manasā, the embodiment of serpent-power. During their long struggle Manasā hurled against him a magical fiery lotus and mustard seed which he countered with a handful of magically potent dust. Then she attacked him with an iron spear, a magic noose consisting of a thousand serpents, and a ladle full of sacred ashes given her by Śiva.

These ashes were especially potent because said to be the *semen virile* of Śiva, and thus were charged with his power and presence.[38] Finally Brahmā and Śiva intervened whereupon Dhanvantari placated Manasā with offerings and prayers. Thus by evoking her benevolent aspect he gained her favour and established 'the pattern for propitiating the fierce form of destruction by acknowledging its irresistible strength. Furthermore, his auspicious vision of the goddess . . . provided the form in which Manasā is to be visualized in meditation and represented in images . . . to avert the peril of poisonous snakes.'[39]

Salves and ointments were used for various purposes, including the removal of demons (*yātus*). Magical ointments were also used by European witches and probably consisted of atropine, a powerful alkaloid found in European plants such as the mandrake, henbane and deadly nightshade (*belladonna*). The outstanding characteristic of atropine is that it is absorbed through the skin, and hence the use of *belladonna* skin plasters for the relief of rheumatism. Salves were also used for the cure of jaundice and disease in general (cf. *RV.* X.97,12); to avert curses, evil dreams, pollution and the 'terrible eye of an enemy'. An efficacious eye salve (*āñjana*) is said to come from the three-peaked (*trikakud*) mountain or from the Yamunā river. The very names of the salve are auspicious, as are the three names of the *kuṣṭha* plant – an example of the protective power inherent in auspicious names. A salve is also used to remove inauspicious portents (*AV.* XIX.44).

Pearl-shell amulets are efficacious against various evils as well as disease. The shell was born of the 'light of lightning' from out of the ocean (*AV.* IV.10); it overcomes demons, disease, misery and *sadānvās* (demonesses).[40] The bones of the gods became living pearl in the waters, and hence a pearl-shell amulet is worn to extend life to a hundred autumns, and to give splendour, strength and protection.

A herb called *arundhatī* is used to heal fractures and reduce inflammation. The bone marrow is commanded to come together, marrow to marrow, joint to joint, and skin to skin (*AV*. IV.12,3–5).[41] The literal meaning of *arundhatī* is 'non-obstructing' and it was probably a quick-growing climbing plant having curative properties. It is associated with various trees including the *plakṣa* (*Ficus infectoria*), *aśvattha*, *khadira* (*Acacia catechu*), *dhava* (*Grislea tomentosa*), *nyagrodha* (banyan) and the *parṇa*. The *arundhatī* herb is said to have fallen from the mouth of Yama's dark brown horse whose saliva covered it. The meaning of the passage is uncertain but as saliva, like blood, is considered to be a focal point of vital power, it would possess magically protective and healing properties. A Babylonian charm reflects this belief and refers to 'the magic which mingles with the spat-forth spittle'; in an ancient Egyptian charm the goddess Isis kneaded Re's spittle, which had fallen on the earth, in to the form of a snake which she placed in Re's path, whereupon the image became a live snake and attacked Re.[42] Spittle was also used in Sumerian atonement rituals to remove the *tabu* of illness. Jesus often made use of spittle when curing men suffering from deafness and blindness (Mark 7:32; 8:23; and John 9:6). Anointing with saliva still plays a part in baptism in the Roman Catholic rite.[43] Galen mentions the power of human saliva to cure snake-bite and scorpion stings. In England, the saliva of a person fasting was used to cure warts, swellings and to remove birthmarks. As late as 1954 a North Oxfordshire woman massaged her child's crooked leg with spittle. After two years the leg became straight although no other treatment had been given.[44]

Some charms are devoted to such trivial matters as increasing the growth of the hair, using a remedy 'plucked from the earth'. *AV*. VI.136 refers to a plant with the epithet *nitatnī* (down-stretcher),[45] probably implying that its roots are deep and strong like those needed for the growth of healthy hair. When the ancient sage Jamadagni wished to increase the growth of his daughter's hair he dug up a particular plant. The ritual (*Kauś*. 31,28) prescribes that a potion made from *nitatnī*, *jīvī*, and *ālākā* plants be poured at daybreak over the head of the patient. He should be dressed in black and eat only black food such as sesame or black beans. Black here symbolizes the new dark hair desired by the patient.

The ever-curative waters, the 'most excellent of physicians', are invoked for relief from various pains in eyes and feet, heartburn and dropsy (*jalodara* 'water-belly') (*AV.* VI.24; *Kauś.* 30,13); the water should be drawn from a stream – but *never* against the current – then warmed with burning thatch and sprinkled on the patient. In common with the Babylonians, ancient Greeks, Egyptians, and Hebrews, the Indians believed some diseases were punishments inflicted by the gods. Dropsy is sent by Varuṇa to wrongdoers, for he is the god of the waters; hence it is called 'Varuṇa's fetter' (*AV.* VII.83). All drowned people and animals belong to him (*ŚBr.* XIII.3.8,5). He also 'seizes' diseases which have been 'washed off' in running water. Varuṇa is called the 'child of the waters' (*apāṁ śiśur*), because he dwells in them in a golden house, even as the mighty Sumerian god Ea always manifested himself in water. The Avestan Apam Napāt also lives in water. The ritual (*Kauś.* 32,14f.) prescribes that a hut be erected on land between the confluence of two rivers. Such a place is doubly potent, being the point where the power of two rivers is combined. The pairing or doubling of gods, godlings, persons or objects was believed to increase their potency. Thus when the *ṛṣi* Bhūtāṁśa Kaśyapa desired offspring his wife said: 'I will bear as many sons as you wish, so long as you praise the gods in pairs' (*Bṛhadd.* VIII,18ff.). The ritual continues with the patient being placed in the hut where he is washed down with water and bunches of grass and rinsed off, the dropsical water being removed by the pure water sprinkled on him (*attractio similium*). A parallel occurs in Babylonian rites where a dough figure of the patient was made and water poured over it to wash away the disease. The Mandaeans of Iraq and Iran also believe that water can wash away sin and impurity from the body, and their 'water-cult, carried on at the very sites of the early water-cults, is at bottom an aboriginal cult, persisting under successive religions and maintaining a continuous and unbroken ritual tradition'.[46]

Fifty-five or seventy-seven sores are said to affect the nape of the neck and ninety-nine the shoulders (*AV.* VI.25). These numbers are often used in charms (see the *sūkta* to Night *AV.* XIX.47,3–5), and are also associated with old German medical charms; Zoroastrians believe that 99,999 diseases plague mankind (*Vendidād*, xxii). To remove the sores fifty-five leaves of the *paraśu* plant (or tree) should be burnt, but first the leaves are boiled to extract the sap, which is smeared on the sores with a wooden stick (spatula?). The smearing is repeated, this time with powdered shell mixed with the saliva of a dog; the patient is then subjected to the bites of leeches, gnats and other insects – this unpleasant treatment being thought to make the disease fly away (*Kauś.* 30,14). The ancient Egyptians also used impure substances to 'repel bad spirits and dissuade them from remaining in diseased persons'.[47] Their pharmacopoeia has been called 'excremental medicine' since they made use of the droppings of pelicans, hippopotami and flies.

Urine (*jālāṣa*) is a remedy for scrofulous sores (*gaṇḍamālā*),[48] a disease designated 'Rudra's arrow' which none the less may be averted by incantations, since both the origin of the illness and the remedy are attributed to Rudra; hence he is called the 'most eminent of physicians' (*RV.* II.33,4). In India, as in ancient Egypt, punitive illnesses could be cured by the god that had caused them.

According to the *Kauś. Sūtra* (31,11), *jālāṣa* is the foam of cow's urine, but Geldner[49] suggests rainwater which is often equated with urine. Urine however seems more likely, especially as cow-urine has been used medicinally since Indo-Iranian times. The *Suś. Saṁ.* (I. pp. 467f.) states that the urine of cows as well as that of buffaloes, goats, sheep, mules, horses, asses and camels may be used medicinally. The sores are moistened with the foam of cow's urine, the remainder being thrown over them and then washed off; the infected parts are also smeared with scourings from the teeth and grass-pollen. Urine, like blood and spittle, has long been thought, in both East and West, to possess magical and healing powers. The Iranians also shared the belief that the urine of cattle possessed powerful purificatory properties. Thus a person possessed by an evil spirit (*druj*) was sprinkled over the whole body with cattle urine, beginning with the head and working downwards until the *druj* was expelled from the toes of the left foot – the last refuge of an evil spirit.

In Europe spells were broken by boiling some of the victim's urine, or by boiling it in combination with his nail-parings or hair, in a sealed room. This practice was based on the belief that when a body had been in contact with another object a mystical relationship was permanently set up, which extended even to used garments. Aubrey,[50] the seventeenth-century diarist, mentions a remedy for fever and ague in which the morning urine was taken from a patient and whilst still warm a perforated egg was boiled in it and then buried in an ant's nest; following which the early recovery of the patient was expected. In England and Wales some people believe that warts, chilblains and chapped hands can be cured by massaging the affected parts with the patient's own urine. In the 1914–18 War urine was used to cure 'trench feet'.

Apacits, probably sores or glandular swellings of the neck,[51] are besought to fly away like birds (*AV*. VI.83). The *apacits* are described as spotted, whitish, black or sometimes red, and as all their names are known they can be rendered powerless. The red *apacit's* 'mother' is described as black (*AV*. VII.74). Thus the ritual (*Kauś*. 32,8–10) prescribes that such sores should be hit by black arrows having bunches of wool tied to their points and shot from a black-stringed bamboo bow.

To remove sores and a disease called *jāyānya* an amulet is fashioned from a lute-string and three fragments of the *vīriṇa* plant (*Andropogon muricatus*) and then tied on the patient (*AV.* VII.76). The amulet combines all the powers of the materials from which it is fashioned. It is not known what disease *jāyānya* was. Bloomfield suggests that it was venereal disease, but Sigerist considers that syphilis was unknown in India until the seventeenth century when it was introduced by Portuguese sailors.

Barley (*yava*) often figured in magic and folk beliefs, and was believed to be a universal remedy (*sarvabhaiṣajyam*), as well as being capable of averting the effects of the Evil Eye and every other calamity. The gods gave the barley plant the sap of every other plant so that it always thrives (*ŚBr.* III.6.1,10). It was a symbol of Indra's mighty thunderbolt (*vajra*) and the guarantor of success (*Tait. Saṁ.* VI.2.5,1f.). Thus barley-gruel (*yavāgū*) was the drink of kings.

A food prepared from barley was also used in penances; the *yāvaka-kṛcchra* being a penance consisting of eating *yāvaka* – a particular food prepared from barley – for specified periods (*Ṛgvidhāna* 9,5). The ancient Hebrews used barley ritually in the meal offering of jealousy.

Pliny's method of transferring boils from a patient to grain was to rub nine grains of barley on each boil, and then throw the grains on a fire. The Greeks offered a kind of porridge made from barley meal (*pelanos*) to the Earth, and to the gods of the underworld and other 'spirits of aversion'.

Barley has been grown since prehistoric times, and was probably the first cereal to be cultivated; in antiquity it was usually the type known as *Hordeum hexastichon*, grains of which have been found in the ruins of pre-dynastic Egypt, and in those of the Indus Valley cities and elsewhere.

Among the herbs mentioned in the *AV.* some not only possessed curative properties but were believed also to possess god-given creative powers, for which they were lauded in prayers. To aquatic plants were attributed the power to remove difficulties; other herbs release one from the bonds of Varuṇa; dispel poison, and counteract or avert witchcraft (*kṛtyā*); whilst other herbs were employed to protect domesticated animals. The 'tigerish amulet of plants' was a particularly powerful amulet invoked to protect the suppliant from the effects of a curse, and from attacks by demons who become terrified when confronted with these potent plants. The Gandharvas and particular animals including the boar, snake, goose know these herbs, and hence the priest calls on them to aid him in his search for them.

An obscure prayer is dedicated to the 'heavenly dog' (perhaps the Sun), and the Kālakāñjas (*AV.* VI.80). The latter were anti-gods (Asuras) who, like the gods, owed their origin to the creator Prajāpati (*Tait. Br.* I.1.2,4ff.). But the Asuras arrogantly aspired to reach heaven by constructing a vast fire-altar. Each Asura placed a brick on the altar, but Indra, in the guise of a brahman, also placed a brick, saying: 'This one, named Citra (the bright one) is for me!' When the top of the altar reached heaven the Asuras began to climb up, but Indra quickly pulled out his brick and the great altar disintegrated. As the Asuras fell they were transformed into spiders, except for two which escaped by flying upwards where they became the two heavenly dogs (the Sun and Moon, or perhaps stars).[52]

Paralysis was said to be inflicted by the beating wings of inauspicious birds, such as crows and pigeons. The cure consisted of rubbing the patient's body with earth from the footprints of a running dog, which represents the mobility desired by the sufferer. The paralysed area is then fumigated by burning an insect taken from the same dog.

The sudden stabbing pains of colic and neuralgia are caused by Rudra's arrows (*AV.* VI.90) which he hurls at his victims. These magical arrows can only be drawn out by priestly incantations. Although the arrows are invisible and divinely superinduced, they cause defilement – a physical 'stain' which can only be 'wiped off' by particular herbs and spells. A spear-shaped amulet is attached to the patient (*Kauś.* 31,7) whose pain resembles that of a wound from a spear thrust, and hence the ailment itself is called *śūla* (spear). Similarly the shaft of Artemis and the 'elf-shots' of European folklore brought plague and other diseases to men and domestic animals. Apollo's arrows were called 'arrows of pestilence' because they inflicted plague on the Libyans and others. Members of the Bergdama tribe of south-west Africa die when their god Gamat shoots arrows at them.

Some wounds are healed with peppercorns (*pippalī*) which are personified. They are said to have 'talked together' saying: 'He who is at present alive shall suffer no harm' (*AV.* VI.109). Similarly plants are said to converse with their king, the Soma plant (*RV.* X.97,17; *Tait. Saṁ.* IV.2,6).

One of the *mātṛnāmāni* charms (those containing the names of the divine mothers) is directed against insanity (*AV.* VI.111). Agni is called upon to calm the lunatic boy who jabbers loudly, and to free him from insanity inflicted by gods or demons. The Apsarasas are also invoked with Indra, Bhaga and other divinities to restore the patient's sanity. The Apsarasas are called 'mind-confusing' – since they and their male companions the Gandharvas cause the madness of love (*RV.* X.95).

For a person possessed by disease-demons the ritual (*Kauś.* 26,29–32) prescribes that fragrant powdered substances mixed with ghee should be offered as a sacrifice, the patient being anointed with the remains. He is then placed at a crossroads (the best place to rid oneself of evil influences) where the disease will be quickly dispersed to the four directions. A basket made of sacred *darbha* grass and containing a coal-pan is placed on his head and the rite repeated. The patient then enters the river *against* the current and throws the powdered substances mixed with ghee into a sieve which symbolizes the manner by which the complaint passes through and away from the sufferer. Sieves or winnowing baskets, in many cultures, are used symbolically to separate the good from the bad, and to sift truth from falsehood, thus the Ndembu of Angola and Western Zambia place divinatory objects in a winnowing basket. The atharvanic rite continues with more of the powdered materials being moistened with ghee and poured into an unannealed clay vessel placed in a tripod wicker-basket which is tied to a tree containing birds' nests to which the unhealthy conditions are transferred. *Darbha* grass itself possesses exorcizing powers; it is also closely associated with sacrificial rites in which it covers the sacred fire-altar, the seat of Agni. Brushes of *darbha* are used to clean the sacrificial area, so removing any defiling matter liable to harbour demonic beings.

Bdellium (*guggulu*),[53] an aromatic gum-resin (*Balsamodendron Roxburghi* or *B. Mukul*), is somewhat similar to myrrh. Because of its refreshing and pleasant scent it is often employed as a charm against numerous ailments (*AV.* XIX.38). Anyone having this odour on his person is protected against curses and disease. *Bdellium* is used especially for sacred fumigations as well as for perfumes and medicine. According to the *Suśruta Saṁhitā* (II. p. 314), it reduces obesity.

Some forms of illness are exorcized by a *varaṇa*-wood amulet which 'wards off' (*vāray*) disease (*AV.* VI.85). *Varaṇa* is believed to possess both medicinal and magical qualities, a notion stemming from its supposed etymology. Similar puns are made in connexion with the *aśvattha, khadira, vibhīdaka*, and other trees.

To attain relief from the penalty for wrong-doing, from distress, from the effects of curses, or to escape the fetters of Varuṇa and Yama, the herbs 'begotten' by Bṛhaspati, the Lord of prayer and of spells, are required (*AV.* VI.96). Another method to obtain relief from the effects of transgressions committed visually, mentally or vocally, whether knowingly or unknowingly, is to invoke the *soma* plant (also used as a pain reliever)[54] to purify everything for his worshippers with *svadhā*—one of the ritual exclamations uttered when making an offering to a deity. These exclamations were regarded as ritual entities and are paralleled by the Greek goddess Ioulô, who was invoked by the *iouloi* (howls) of Demeter's devotees. Similarly the ancient Greek ritual cries, *iacchos* and *bacchos* and others, were later personified as gods. The Sumerian deity Alala was created from the *alala* or ritual wail; the Basque hero Lelo, often lamented in folk-songs, is also 'a projection of the *lelo* or dirge'.[55]

AV. VI.113 is designed to obtain release from Grāhi, who enters a patient as subtly as an image enters the surface of a mirror (*Suś. Saṁ*. III. p. 376). Grāhi personifies the unspecified sin or sins committed in the distant past by the gods and not by man as in Christianity. Because the gods transferred their sins to the mysterious being called Trita, they are invoked to remove the sins of their worshippers by the appropriate mantras.

Although Vedic medicine failed to appreciate the influence of the mind on disease and vice versa, this was later achieved in India by systematized yogic training and techniques, which required physiological knowledge. The establishment of Buddhism was an important factor in increasing medical knowledge, the monks being expected to cure their sick brethren as well as laymen and animals. Wealthy members of the laity and rulers provided hospitals and medical care for the poor, and for animals.

Many of the ancient remedies and charms having passed into Hindu classical medicine were then carried to countries influenced by Hinduism and Buddhism. Although many centuries have passed since the compilation of the *AV*. modern man, like his Vedic counterpart, still desires health, prosperity and longevity.

TWO

Charms for longevity

The desire for longevity is common to most cultures, and in some it became extended to a desire for eternal life, but to the Hindu and Buddhist there is no 'complete immortality' since the gods and the worlds with all their inhabitants must by their very nature die.

The Vedic ideal was a pleasant, healthy life-span of a 'hundred autumns' (*RV.* VII.66,16; X.18,5); its attainment necessitated the propitiation of a number of deities, including Yama (the Avestan Yima), believed to be the first man to die and who later became the ruler of the dead; Mṛtyu, the personification of Death (also called Antaka, the Ender); and Nirṛti, the goddess of misery, decay and destruction.

According to the *Ṛgvidhāna* (I.11,2ff.) longevity can be attained by performing certain rites, including 'muttering' verses which contain the word *śam* (which means to appease, pacify or calm), and mantras which include the word *svasti*, and the *trivṛt* verses, i.e., the nine verses of *RV.* IX.11 addressed to Soma Pavamāna. The suppliant immerses himself in water and mutters stanzas containing the words *śuddha* (cleansed, pure) and 'water', and recites the 'sin-effacing' *sūkta*.

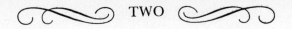

A *sūkta* (*RV.* III.53) praising Indra is traditionally held to bestow longevity and prosperity, but others are also believed to be efficacious. None the less, it was essential to laud the immortal fire, personified as Agni, for he alone of the gods was always immortal, existing in the heat and light of the sun, in lightning and in the fire latent in every tree, whose wood provides the fire-sticks (*araṇi*) which, after the upper stick is twirled or rotated in the socket of the lower, seems magically to produce fire. Not only was Agni present in the sacrificial fire, but also in the domestic fire from which he warmed and cheered the household, warded off wild animals and the hosts of hostile spirits, and hence he was regarded as the demon destroyer *par excellence* who is invoked to 'burn up our enemies whom fiends protect' (*RV.* I.12,3) and to 'consume all demons and sorcerers, and every devouring fiend' (I.36,20). It was customary for a priest to carry fire whilst circumambulating sacrificial objects including the victim, the post (*yūpa*) and the offerings, all of which required protection from hostile influences. At the conclusion of funerary rites the mourners also used fire to ward off death-causing powers which might be attracted to those who had taken part in the ceremony. Similar fears were common in Europe where black was *de rigueur* at funerals, the idea being that demons attracted to the corpse would fail to see the mourners and hence would not attack them.

According to Indian tradition Suśruta, son of the Vedic priest and singer Viśvāmitra, led a group of *ṛṣis* to Divodāsa's hermitage and begged him to teach them the secret of longevity, thus enabling them to heal and to prolong their own lives and also the lives of others. Divodāsa was the incarnation of Dhanvantari, the physician of the gods. He agreed to help the *ṛṣis* and taught them the Āyurveda (the Veda of life) as originally handed down by the Creator Brahmā. This attribution of divine origin to the *Suśruta Saṁhitā* greatly enhanced its authority and importance.

One of the many ways of attaining longevity was the wearing of a gold amulet (*AV.* I.35), gold symbolizing immortality, incorruptibility and light, and hence its association with the eternal sun, the embodiment of immortality. Gold was said to have originated from Indra's semen (*ŚBr.* XII.7.1,7); or from that of the horse immolated at the *aśvamedha* (horse sacrifice). The sacrificial horse is probably a theriomorphic form of the Creator (Prajāpati), who is equated with Agni whose semen also turned into gold (*ŚBr.* II.1.1,5). Elsewhere, gold is said to be born from the immortal fire, thus one who wears gold will never die prematurely (*AV.* XIX.26).

Legend states that the Dākṣāyaṇas, the descendants of Dakṣa (the embodiment of ritual skill), bound a golden amulet on a man called Śatānīka, who desired long life. The amulet, called the 'first-born force of the gods', also bestows splendour and strength on the wearer, as well as protecting him from demons and *piśācas*. The Bible describes God as surrounded by a wondrous sheen of gold, the lustre of divinity; but the Mexican Indians, to whom gold was no rarity, called it the 'faeces of the gods'.[1] The brilliancy and strength of the waters and the tremendous strength of forest trees are also inherent in the golden amulet, and from it these qualities are transmitted to the wearer.

A salve (*āñjana*) amulet is employed ritually (*Kauś.* 58,8; *AV.* IV.9) to ensure the longevity of a Vedic pupil after his initiation. It is called 'all-healing', and an 'extender of lifetime'. It is also a protection against witchcraft and the dread Evil Eye (*AV.* XIX.44–5). Pearl-shell amulets are also life-prolonging (*AV.* IV.10,4).

To ensure that a child shall be long lived the friendly god Mitra is invoked to protect it. He is an Āditya and thus a solar god. The Indo-Iranian Mithra, the equivalent of the Vedic Mitra, was also a bringer of rain, good health and longevity, because of his association with the life-giving sun. Mitra never injures the animate or inanimate (*ŚBr.* V.3.2,6–7), and hence to gaze steadfastly at an object 'with the eye of Mitra' will annihilate any evil influences adhering to it; a steadfast gaze is a ritual technique to appease a particular object.[2] Jara (old age personified) is implored to allow a boy to grow and to protect him from harm by the 'hundred deaths' (*AV.*

II.28) – probably a reference to the fact that the child might die in any of the hundred years which make up the ideal life-span. The hundred and first death, sometimes mentioned in texts, refers to natural death by fluxion of time, the extra one represents Totality, the completion of one lifetime. Father Heaven and Mother Earth are also invoked to allow him to live in the 'lap of Aditi' (the mother of Mitra), for a hundred winters. Whilst reciting the charm his parents pass him to and fro thrice, then feed him 'dumplings' prepared with ghee (clarified butter); the latter is always associated with abundance, life and fertility because of its fatty nature and golden colour which associates it with the sun. The *RV.* (IV.58,1ff.) equates ghee with ambrosia (*amṛta*), the elixir of immortality. If ghee is cooked a hundred times with an aromatic root called *vacā*, and taken daily, one's life is extended to five centuries (*Suś. Saṁ.* II. p. 527).

For relief from disease and for the attainment of longevity the priest says: 'I release you by [means of] the oblation, from unknown disease (*ajñātayakṣma*) and from royal *yakṣma* (*rājayakṣma*)' (*AV.* III.11). Even if a patient is near the end of his life, or in the very presence of Death himself, the powerful 'thousand-eyed' (*sahasrākṣa*) oblation is still powerful enough to remove him from the 'lap of destruction' (personified as the goddess Nirṛti). A thousand eyes is a divine attribute, here associated with this oblation which is itself regarded as an entity capable of bestowing longevity.

An amulet of *pūtudru* wood also gives immunity from an early death (*AV.* VIII.2). To ensure magically the suppliant's longevity the priest breathes over him with the 'life-breath of two-footed and four-footed creatures' – a notion deriving from the observation that when embers or a newly kindled fire are blown on they immediately revive.[3] Thus the suppliant is prevented from disappearing into 'mist and darkness' and 'fading away' into death. The Creator Prajāpati infused life into man by breathing over him, as the Old Testament God Yahweh animated clay by his breath.

According to the *First Gospel of the Infancy of Jesus Christ*, the child Jesus similarly animated clay birds (ch. XV.1ff.). The Greek goddess Athene breathed life into the clay figure moulded by Prometheus. Gaster[4] points out that breath is everywhere a synonym for 'self' such 'as the Hebrew *nephesh*, the Sanskrit *ātman*, the Greek *pneuma*, the Latin *anima* and the Slavonic *duch* (whence Gypsy *duk*) . . . the West Australian *waug* . . . the Javanese *nawa*, and . . . the word *piuts* in the language of the Netela Indians of California'. At the end of the prayer homage is paid to the eye of Death (personified) and to its breath, because that which is beyond man's control must be propitiated.

The *pūtudru* amulet drives away all Yama's messengers who are constantly on the look-out for victims; it also drives away Arāti (the personification of ill-will, grudge, or spite), as well as Nirṛti, Grahī, and *piśācas* and *rākṣasas*. The immortal Agni Jātavedas is begged to give 'life-breaths' to his worshippers that they may live forever with him. If a man or an animal has this rite performed for them, each is assured of protection for life.

Sometimes the worshipper addresses his own breath to ensure its continuing beneficent presence within himself (*AV*. XI.4), and gives 'a comprehensive description of the functions and potency of life-breath in both macrocosm and microcosm'.[5] The above formula is also employed in rites for averting evil (*mahā-śānti*); to propitiate the malignant planet Saturn; and in the ceremony when a brahmin teacher invests a pupil with the sacred thread (*yajñopavīta*).

Healing power is said to reside in the breath (*AV*. XI.4,9) but remains latent until 'stimulated' according to the established magical ritual. Zimmer suggests that the rhythmical monotony of incantations probably indicates that their recital was also accompanied by a rhythmic breathing technique intended both to evoke and to propitiate breath, so essential to life.[6]

Breath is the paramount principle of nature, incorporating both the negative and positive aspects of existence, and thus ranks with the highest Hindu divinities. But it may sometimes appear as fever, or as Death incarnate, when it becomes the vehicle for the spirit in its final hour. As the immortal breath leaves the body it gathers up the sensual and psychic forces of 'him who speaks truth' and conveys his spirit to the realm of the gods. In the folklore of many countries it was thought that if the last breath of a dying person was 'caught' by a relative it would transmit his personality to the succeeding generation. For this reason Jacob kissed the dying Abraham.[7]

The ancient and complex techniques of yoga are primarily concerned with breath-control (*prāṇāyāma*) which was conducive *inter alia* to good health and hence to longevity. The *Śvetāśvatara Upaniṣad* (2.12) states that one who has obtained a body made out of the 'fire of yoga' will never be affected by sickness, old age or death. Yogic adepts such as the historical Buddha and the Siddhas ('perfected ones') were able to postpone indefinitely the hour of their deaths.

To ensure that a newborn child shall live a full span of a hundred years, the father engages five priests, each of whom sits at one of the four cardinal points, but the position of the fifth is unspecified. Perhaps he stood and thus was able to breathe directly down on the babe. Each of the other priests in turn breathes on the infant, first by the one sitting on the eastern side, and proceeding in the auspicious sun-wise direction. If priests are not available the father himself may perform the ceremony by breathing over the child whilst walking round him in the sun-wise direction (*ŚBr.* XI.8.3,6).

Another longevity-bestowing amulet was the *astṛta* ('unsubdued', literally 'not laid low') (*AV.* XIX.46 and V.28), which consisted of single pieces of gold, silver and iron, but in *AV.* VI.133 a girdle (*mekhalā*) was employed. The girdle itself was also invoked to give courage, wisdom, fervour and power equal to that of Indra. The suppliant prays that even as the ancient *ṛṣis* bound on the girdle of longevity, so may it also encircle him and bestow long life. The closed circle gave rise to a feeling of protection, a focusing of power, and of continuity and immortality, thus the magician stands in a circle whilst performing magical rites. Inside the circle is a different kind of reality from that outside, and thus the magician is safe from the attacks of external malevolent forces – a notion deriving from Sumerian and Babylonian magical practices.[8] The elaborate, heavily ornamented girdles depicted on pre-Mauryan terracotta figures of fertility goddesses also had ritual and magical connotations as well as that of continuity.[9]

A number of other amulets also impart longevity, including one of ivory and elephant's hair wrapped in gold wire (*Kauś.* 13,1–3), both objects connected with a long-lived animal. Rings made of elephant hair are often seen in England and are worn to give superior strength, or to achieve a desired object. The latter is similar to the Indian belief that the elephant-headed god Gaṇeśa overcomes all obstacles.

Sometimes homage is paid to 'Immortal Death' (personified) who is implored to grant the suppliant long life (*AV.* VIII.1), a plea which requires the appeasement of Death for having temporarily lost a victim. By 'divine utterance' (i.e., a mantra or prayer) man is saved from the clutches of Nirṛti the goddess of destruction. It is particularly dangerous for the living to yearn for the return of the dead because it may attract the attention of the black and the brindle dogs[10] of Yama who roam the road to the region of the dead looking for potential victims. The household fires are also invoked for protection. The priest prays that the suppliant's breath and strength shall not leave him, nor the convulsion that draws the jaws together (lockjaw) attack him, nor the demon that tears out the tongue; nor shall the women with dishevelled hair, the 'evil-wailers', wail for him, nor Death, destruction and *yakṣma* (disease) draw near him. The 'evil-wailers' naturally portend evil (*AV.* XI.2,11). They were probably similar to the professional Hebrew wailing women, who during burials sang a sort of dirge, at the same time sprinkling dust and ashes on their heads (Isaiah 3:26, etc.), and to the mourning women lacerating their breasts who are depicted on the sarcophagus of King Ahiram of Byblos (twelfth century BC) now in the National Museum, Beirut.

Just as the primitive urge to survive was succeeded by the desire for a long life, so by the end of the Vedic period (c. eighth century BC) it was in turn succeeded by a desire for a kind of immortality lasting thousands of years but finally ending with the destruction of the world at the end of the age. Immortality was envisaged in a number of metaphysical theories, including successive rejuvenations, usually carried out by the gods as a boon to their favoured worshippers, or as successive rebirths in which the individual was purged of all imperfections, whereupon supreme knowledge was attained. The latter, however, was not to be achieved by the performance of rites, or the use of charms, though these continued to be relied upon by the masses. Another method of ensuring immortality was the ritual cooking of the consecrated *brahmaudana* (rice-porridge) which enabled the worshipper to live in Yama's world with the gods and the *soma*-drinking heavenly minstrels (*gandharvas*) (*AV.* IV.34,3). (Compare Jesus' words to the Jews: 'I say unto you, Except ye eat the flesh of the Son of man and drink his blood, ye have not life in yourselves. He that eateth my flesh and drinketh my blood hath eternal life', John 6:53ff.). The spirits of the dead were thought to rise from the (immortal) cooked offering and to be united with their children in Yama's world. Here the rice-dish and its contents represent the conclusion of earthly life, which is to be followed by a happy hereafter, and so the worshippers pray: 'let old age commit us to death; then we may be united with the cooked [offering]' (*AV.* XII.3,55).

One of the early Upaniṣads, the *Chāndogya* (2,11ff.; 4,11ff.), states that the reward for the acquisition of sacred knowledge is longevity, fame and many cattle, but a later Upaniṣad, the *Kaṭha* (I.26ff.), points out that only by the abandonment of all worldly attachments, including even the desire for longevity, will immortality be attained.

THREE

Charms relating mainly to women

The two main classes of charms used in women's rites are first, those to ensure a suitable husband and children; second, those relating to exorcizing demonic forces, counteracting the effects of curses, eliminating rivals and fulfilling individual wishes and ambitions. Though many charms were employed by or on behalf of women, some were used by men seeking to gain some advantage in affairs of the heart.

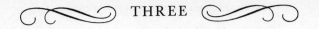

Many of these charms reflect important aspects of human nature and show that the high position accorded early woman was largely because of her procreative ability, anciently regarded as magical and unconnected with the copulative act, a belief common among some African and Australian tribes as late as the nineteenth century. But when man became aware that without him woman's magical power ceased to function, her unique status also ceased – at least in the estimation of man – hence the many restrictions and the lower status accorded her in patriarchal cultures, her high status being maintained only among matriarchal tribes. The reason for many of the charms relating to women in Vedic India was naturally bound up with her position *vis-à-vis* man, a relationship subject to minor changes, according to the reciprocal influences of Aryans and indigenes, until finally Aryan patriarchal bias became dominant. This is confirmed in one of the Indian accounts of creation contained in the *Bṛhad Āraṇyaka Upaniṣad* 6,4 (c. 1000 BC), which relates that the Creator Prajāpati made woman for man, as the Hebrew Yahweh created Eve for Adam, though both the Indian and the Hebrew accounts indicate that women should be respected. The same Upaniṣad equates various parts of a woman's body with the all-important rite of sacrifice and with the sacrificial utensils. (In Indo-Iranian cultures the sacrifice is closely associated with the creative act.) The woman's lap is equated with the altar, her hair with the sacrificial grass, her vulva with the altar fire. The last implies the heat of sexual desire, thus a man whose wife has been unfaithful performs a rite cursing the seducer to become impotent and devoid of merit, saying: 'You have made a libation in my fire! I deprive you of your breath, your sacrifices, meritorious deeds and hopes. . .' (*Bṛhad Āraṇyaka Upaniṣad* 6.4,12). The same work also mentions a curious form of birth control. As a man embraces a woman he inhales and then exhales and says: 'With the power of the semen I give you, with that power I reclaim it from you.'

The *Ṛgveda* has an ambivalent attitude to women. They were important enough to take part in sacrificial sessions with their husbands (I.72,5; 83,3, etc.) – a right they lost in post-Vedic times – and were the legitimate booty of victorious campaigns (IV.17,16). Occasionally they are praised (V.61,6); but elsewhere are said to be undisciplined and of little intelligence (VIII.33,17). A sacrificer's wife is impure below the navel, therefore she has to wrap herself in a cloth or skirt made of purifying *kuśa* grass (*ŚBr.* V.2.1,8). In the *aśvamedha* (horse sacrifice) a number of women were given as *dakṣiṇā* to the priests after the *udavasānīyā* (the closing offering) (*ŚBr.* XIII.5.4,27).

The strengthening patriarchal bias resulted in women being generally condemned to illiteracy, though some exceptions are recorded like Gārgī Vācaknavī (*Bṛhad Āraṇyaka Upaniṣad* 8,1ff.). But the majority were denied direct access to the vast store of Indian religious works, and were limited to popular stories chiefly from the *Mahābhārata* and the Purāṇas, which, as they were unable to read, had to be retailed to them. Such conditions persisted for many centuries and only in recent years have women been granted cultural opportunities similar to those available to men.

But women's problems were not entirely overlooked, though the solution to some of these were not always free from male self-interest. Some atharvanic charms were designed to enhance the physical attractions of women. One of the most important is the removal of blemishes on the skin, regarded as the work of demons, some of whom were named. Several divinities were invoked for aid, including Savitar, Varuṇa, Mitra, Aryaman, each being assigned to remove particular unsightly marks. The goddess Anumati (the personification of divine favour) is especially invoked since women's happiness was her motive in creating them (*AV.* I.18). To remove blemishes the ritual prescribes sprinkling the woman's face with water, the purifier *par excellence*, followed by an offering of chaff from a vessel of *palāśa* wood, the residue being poured on the ground to placate the *rākṣasas* and other demons responsible for the blemishes. Then more chaff, wood shavings and other worthless materials are placed on her left foot (the left in ritual and folklore always being the inauspicious side). The worthless materials represent the blemishes which are then symbolically washed off the woman. Each person is said to be born with 101 marks on the body, some auspicious and some not. Eye-brows which meet were deemed especially unlucky.

Although marriage was considered to be important there are few references to it in the first nine books (*maṇḍalas*) of the *Ṛgveda*, which suggests a lack of rules relating to it and a considerable amount of freedom of choice in the selection of a wife or husband.[1] The only marriage prohibition mentioned or implied was the marriage of Aryans with Dasyus (aboriginals), Indra being implored to protect the Aryan colour (*ārya-varṇa*) (*RV.* III.34,9).

Having done all in her power to ensure her own attractiveness, a girl had then to ensure that her future husband should also be suitable. To this end she enlists the aid of Agni, and also that of the gods Soma, Brahmā, Aryaman and Dhātar. She is then given a rice and sesame pudding, and gold, *bdellium* and other precious objects are placed on a clay altar, the clay being taken from a cave inhabited by wild animals. The gold and other objects are anointed with dregs of ghee and then given her to wear. At night she makes an offering of rice and barley from a copper vessel[2] to Jāmi, goddess of femininity or maternity. She then walks round the vessel, keeping it on her right, after which she is washed on the western side of the fire, and oracles are consulted to ascertain whether or not she will obtain a desirable husband (*AV.* II.36; *Kauś.* 34,12ff.).

To secure a woman's love the aid of the two Aśvins is invoked (*AV.* II.30). They are mythically associated with marriage because they wooed Sūryā, the daughter of the Sun on behalf of Soma (*RV.* X.85,14). The ritual (*Kauś.* 35,21ff.) prescribes the placing of an arrow (a phallic symbol)[3] between two chips from a tree and two pieces from a creeper growing on it. A concoction containing *sthakara* powder, salve, *kuṣṭha*, sweet-wood and a stalk of grass broken by the wind, is mixed with melted butter and used to anoint the girl. *Kuṣṭha* is also used with nard and *madugha* to make a salve by which a woman may be made subject to a man's will. When the woman was anointed with the salve it aroused her desires. Another method is for a man to boil rice-grains which he breaks with his finger-nails and crushes. He then forms them into an effigy of the desired woman whilst concentrating solely on her. The effigy is anointed with sesamum oil and then torn limb from limb, starting with the feet. With the exclamation *phaṭ* they are thrown into the fire until the whole effigy is destroyed except for the region of the heart which should be placed on the suppliant's own heart whilst he mutters a specified mantra which will draw the woman to him (*Ṛgvidhāna* III.19,4ff.;20,1ff.). The *bīja*-mantra *phaṭ* has long been used ritually as an aggressive mantra. To the Indian ear it implies the sound of breaking or bursting and superhuman power, and thus is eminently suitable for use in magic formulas for destructive ends.

Kāma,[4] the god of love, is invoked by a man seeking to attract a woman (*AV.* III.25). The ritual (*Kauś.* 35,22ff.) prescribes *inter alia* that the lover should press the woman with his thumb – here perhaps representing the phallus.[5] Then twenty-one pieces of *kūdī* wood with the thorns pointing eastwards are put on the fire. For three days thrice daily the suppliant burns *kuṣṭha* (an aromatic plant) dipped in butter, and for three nights sleeps face downwards on his mattress. A tripod filled with warm water is fastened to the foot of the bed, the water of which he moves with his big toes; he pierces a clay effigy of the woman through the heart with an owl-feathered black arrow, to bring her into his power.

Fragrant plants and sweet-smelling substances are frequently used in love-spells and potions, especially the 'honey-born' *madugha* plant which attracts women to men (*AV.* I.34).[6] Recently in the USA the dragon's blood (a gum used in wood-staining) love-potion has been revived. This potion enjoyed great popularity during the nineteenth century in the poorer parts of London. If it is burned on a Friday it will rekindle the affections of a former lover. Navajo love-beads are also being sold in many American cities.

To gain a man's love a number of goddesses were invoked, including Anumati, goddess of favour and consent; Āküti, goddess of plans and schemes; and Indrāṇī, the personification of marital bliss (*AV.* VI.130 to 132). These three charms are employed in the ritual (*Kauś.* 36,13–14) which prescribes that beans be thrown on to the head of the desired man, whose effigy is then placed facing the suppliant; lighted arrows (representing the phallus) are then thrown around the figure. In popular charms beans represent the testicles and are also regarded as aphrodisiacs; hence they, together with honey, salt, meat and brandy, are prohibited foods[7] for one about to perform religious rites.

Having won a man's love, the woman had to hold his affection, which necessitated the use of a particularly highly-scented plant which would cause him to return to her no matter where he was. This notion is based on the myth of the Āsurī who, by means of a fragrant plant, seduced Indra away from the gods.

As marriage was considered to be only a prelude to the procreation of offspring – sons being specially desired – a number of rites were designed to achieve this aim,[8] one of which involved the cooking and preparation of the consecrated rice-porridge (*brahmaudana* or *odana*) which was distributed to the priests at sacrificial sessions. This offering is closely connected with thaumaturgy and therefore could be used ritually for good or bad ends. When the goddess Aditi desired sons, she cooked a *brahmaudana*. According to the account in the *Tait. Saṁ.* VI.5,6, she presented the concentrated food to the Sādhya gods who dwelt in the region between heaven and earth. They gave her the potent remains (which represent continuity) to eat, whereupon she became pregnant and gave birth to four of the Ādityas (sun-gods). She cooked another *brahmaudana* so that she might have even stronger children but produced only an egg which miscarried. A third cooked offering was made, this time for the Ādityas, who said: 'Let us choose a boon; let him who shall be born hence be one of us . . .', whereupon the Āditya Vivasvant was born. Thus the cooked offering also represents or symbolizes seed as stated in the *ŚBr.* XIII.1.1,4. A brahmin who desires offspring should *inter alia* pour ghee into a fire whilst uttering *RV.* II.32,4–8 which calls upon the two goddesses Rākā and Sinīvālī for sons. After eating the remains of the oblation he will obtain numerous offspring (*Ṛgvidhāna* I.30,3f.); the same work (II.16,2) states that a person desirous of offspring should regularly worship the wives of the gods (*devapatnīs*) with rice oblations, and the remains should be given to the woman desiring sons. A curious belief in the Purāṇas states that sons are conceived on even nights and girls on odd nights. The Indians, Greeks, Romans, Jews, ancient Germans and Slavs thought that the male foetus was to be found in the right side of the womb, and the female in the left – the inauspicious side.

The overwhelming desire for sons ensured that great care was taken of pregnant women, they being especially vulnerable to demonic attacks which could cause still-birth or a deformed embryo. A post-Vedic work, the *Mahābhārata*, describes such demons who sometimes eat infants. They live in the lying-in room for about ten nights. A snake-demoness may penetrate the womb and destroy the embryo, the woman then gives birth to a snake, or the mother of the Apsarasas removes the foetus and the woman loses her child. The demoness Pūtanā kills children who suck her poisonous milk (*Bhāgavata Purāṇa* X.6). But there are some beneficent goddesses who help to counteract the power of maleficent beings. Among them is Ṣaṣṭhī, a folk-goddess of ancient and medieval India, who personifies the sixth day after the birth of the child who henceforth is in her care. Later Ṣaṣṭhī merged with Śrī, the goddess of good fortune.

Great care was taken to protect pregnant women from unpleasant sights, and a fire was kept burning day and night in their rooms to repel demons.

By the third month of pregnancy a woman was expected to divine the sex of the embryo. One method was for her youngest child (with averted gaze) to touch her body and, according to the grammatical gender of the part touched, the sex of the unborn child would be either male or female. During the third month the husband played his part by performing the *puṁsavana* rite to ensure that the embryo would be male.[9] When the birth occurred, but before the umbilical cord was cut, the father breathed on the boy three times and invoked the blessings of the Vedas. The triple exhalation is similar to the early Roman Catholic method of invoking the Holy Spirit.[10] A godling called Piṅga protected the child during the actual delivery[11] and was implored to ensure that it was male. Other methods of ascertaining a child's sex before birth are given in the post-Vedic *Agni Purāṇa* (CXLI, 3–5). To ensure easy parturition the gods Aryaman and Pūṣan were invoked, Aryaman because he controls marriage contracts, finds husbands for girls and ensures domestic harmony, and Pūṣan (from the root *puṣ*, 'to nourish') because he bestows fertility (*AV.* I.11) and thus ensures food for the child. (Aryaman's Avestan counterpart is Airyaman.) One of the great Zoroastrian Prayers addresses him as 'Desirable Airyaman'. This prayer is the most powerful mantra against sickness and has been employed for this purpose down the centuries. It forms part of the Zoroastrian wedding ceremony when guests are entertained.[12] The officiant implores the gods to 'open the woman' so that the embryo can be freed. Similarly Leah's womb was opened by the Lord (Gen. 29:31). The two minor Vedic goddesses, Sūṣaṇā and Biṣkalā, were also implored to 'loosen' the womb and allow the embryo to emerge. The names of these divinities indicate their functions: Sūṣaṇā probably being derived from the root *sū*, 'to set in motion', 'bring forth', or 'vivify',[13] and Biṣkalā, indicating fertility, such as that of the sow, which in turn is associated with her masculine counterpart the hog (*biṣkala*), noted for its virility.

All folk-cultures have their own particular accouchment customs, but a curious one is ascribed to eighteenth-century Welsh midwives, who were supposed to have used toasted cheese to entice a reluctant embryo from the womb![14]

The ritual (*Kauś.* 33,1ff.) employs the above charm (i.e., *AV.* I.11) in a long and complex ceremony for safe delivery, but as much of it appears to have little connexion with the main intention of the rite, only the relevant part is given here. Four portions of dregs of ghee are poured into a pail, and four *muñja*-reeds are placed on the woman's head pointing eastwards, with the sheaths of the *muñja* facing westward. If they break, it portends danger. *Muñja* (*Saccharum muñja*) is a tall sedge-like grass often used in ritual. It is likened to a womb from which the fire (*agni*) was to be born (*ŚBr.* VI.6.1,23). The woman is washed with warm water, beginning with her right-hand braid of hair, and the wooden joints of the house loosened, a symbolic act believed to loosen the embryo. The untying of knots also serves the same purpose and was customary in many parts of the world, including Persia, the Near East, among the Pacific peoples, and in parts of rural Europe. To prevent a premature birth, the Earth, the embryo of existence, is called upon to guard the foetus until it attains maturity (*AV.* VI.17).

Before being given the breast the baby boy must undergo the 'vivifying' (*āyuṣya*) and 'first-feeding' (*prāśana*) ceremonies, as well as the *medhājanana* which gives intellectual powers.[15] Ground-rice mixed with honey and called *caru* is usually offered to the gods, but in this ceremony it is given to the baby to ensure the development of his intelligence and that he will live the full life-span of one hundred years (*Ṛgvidhāna* IV.19,1ff.).

To obtain a son having a particular complexion the parents were required to eat specific foods. For a pale-complexioned son, rice cooked with milk and ghee was prescribed; for one with a swarthy complexion, rice boiled with water and ghee; for a learned son able to repeat all the Vedas and attain old age, meat – either veal or beef; for a learned daughter, rice boiled with sesamum and ghee. Such distinctions indicate that racial integration had reached an advanced stage over a large part of northern India.

A charm of the *cātanāni* class (*AV.* II.14) was used to prevent a miscarriage by exorcizing the demonesses called *sadānvās*, who attack men, women and cattle. To prevent miscarriage, the above charm was recited whilst the officiating priest poured dregs of ghee into pots of water placed in three huts, each having doors facing east and west. The woman concerned was dressed in black (the colour of Nirṛti). More ghee dregs were poured on to a piece of lead placed on a *palāśa* leaf, on which the woman stands before being washed down; she then leaves her black garment in the first hut, thus symbolically ridding herself of misfortune. Finally, the priest sets fire to the hut. More rites are carried out in the other two huts. On returning home she is given rice-cakes, symbolizing fertility – as does the rice thrown over brides at European weddings.

Miscarriage and still-birth were attributed to various kinds of demons, but a remedy called *baja*, perhaps a species of white or red mustard,[16] expelled the demons which hide between the thighs of pregnant woman. The seeds of red mustard, when poured into a fire, subdue all maleficent forces (*Ṛgvidhāna* II.10,3). *Baja* also drives away demons, whose feet have the heels in front and the toes pointing backwards, and who emerged either from the dust of the threshing floor or from dung-smoke. Some women who died in childbirth became evil spirits with similarly 'reversed' feet.[17]

Another way of avoiding a miscarriage was for the pregnant woman to pour a burnt offering and ghee into the fire whilst muttering *RV*. X.162, addressed to Agni the demon slayer, imploring him to exterminate everything inimical to the womb and the embryo. This *sūkta* is recognized 'as a concentrating prayer for children [prematurely] issuing from the womb' (*Bṛhadd.*VIII.65; *Ṛgvidhāna* IV.17,1ff.).[18]

Another class of spells relates to the overcoming of a woman's rivals, one of the most vitriolic being that given in *AV*. I.14, which is a reminder that if hell has no fury like that of a woman scorned, it has also no fury like that of a woman in danger of being supplanted by a rival. An incantation is uttered to destroy the rival's luck (*bhaga*) in affairs of love. The term *bhaga* means both 'fortune' and 'vulva', but in the context of sexual rivalry it refers to 'vulva', and the spell is intended to destroy the rival's fecundity. Furthermore, she is also cursed to become the bride of Yama, the ruler of the dead (cf. the modern English imprecation: 'Drop dead!'). If death should be unduly delayed the curse condemns her to remain unmarried in the parental home. To ensure this the ritual (*Kauś.* 36,15ff.) prescribes that parts of her garland, tooth-twig and hair be placed in a piece of hide from a sacrificial cow. The hide and other objects (representing the rival's good fortune) are then buried in a cavity or in a mortar under three stones. The rest of the garland is ground up and buried under three stones with three tufts of hair, each tied with black thread. Subsequently, they are dug up, and with that act the rival is deprived of her good fortune, merits, fecundity and possessions.

Some atharvanic charms are designed to avert, allay or overcome jealousy, whilst others give full scope to jealous impulses and the desire to overcome or harm rivals. Jealousy, as well as hatred and rage, were regarded as separate entities which afflicted both men and women. But in primitive times it seems that jealousy was almost unknown. Together with envy, it seems to increase with the growth of culture.

To prevent a rival bearing a male child *AV.* VII.34 is employed, but *AV.* VII.35 is used if the intention is to make her completely barren. The latter charm invokes Jātavedas (Agni) to overpower rivals and to thrust back those unborn; to reverse the upper and lower parts of the womb; and to render the rival as barren (*asū*) as a mule. The ritual (*Kauś.* 36,33f.) prescribes that the urine of a she-mule be rubbed between two stone discs (symbolizing inability to conceive) and then put into the food or cosmetics of the rival. In other charms against rivals (*AV.* VII.113; see also III.18), a poisonous plant called *bāṇāparṇī*, 'arrow-feather', was used and commanded to injure her vagina with its roughness or spikiness. So strong was the belief in the efficacy of mantras or words of power, that it was believed that the roughness of the plant would be conveyed to the hated woman whose lover would then avoid her as a bull avoids a barren cow.

Indrāṇī, the consort of Indra, is said to have uttered the *sapatnībādhanam* (*RV.* X.145) as a means of overcoming rivals, thus it is similarly employed by jealous women. This typically atharvanic 'hymn' mentions an unspecified plant, having expanded or erect leaves, which is invoked to blow away the rival wife and make the suppliant's husband cleave only to her.

Indra and Indrāṇī embody the ideal of marital bliss and harmony, thus special oblations are offered to them by those desiring matrimonial happiness, and also to the divine Tvaṣṭṛ who fashions men and women, gives them happiness, and increases their life-span a thousandfold (*AV.* VI.78).

Much Indian literature shows women as being more resolute, energetic and passionate than men. Women often take the lead in the old Indian love-tales. These tales also influenced the old French love stories where even high-class women often throw themselves into the arms of heroic strangers. From France these stories entered the literature of the German Middle Ages.[19]

The Indian poets say that the *kurabaka* covers itself with blooms when a woman clasps it, the *tilaka* blooms when she looks at it, the *aśoka* when touched by her foot, the mango when touched by her hand, the *keśava* when sprinkled with intoxicants from her mouth (*Raghuvaṁśa* IX.33; *Gauḍavaha* 1087, etc.). The first is beautifully depicted on the Bhārhut stūpa where Culakoka Devatā is shown with her left arm and leg entwined round a tree.

Girls, especially virgins, were lucky and were often called in for divining by means of dice; a faithful wife could also give magic help to her husband by influencing his luck at dice.

FOUR

Charms pertaining to royalty

The nomadic Aryan tribes who conquered north-western India during the second millennium BC had no kings, only chiefs or tribal leaders. But in the course of time, when the Aryans led a more settled existence, kingdoms were established which required men with the qualities of leadership, military skill, organizing ability and courage. The establishment of the early kingdoms was achieved not only by force of arms, but also by a firm belief in the efficacy of magical ritual and incantations. The many benefits to be derived from a strong, steadfast ruler are often referred to. The king is to be like the mighty war-god Indra and to hold 'kingship' in his grasp; his strength is further increased by the power of the oblations he offers, and the *soma*-sacrifice which makes him a conqueror (*RV.* X.173;174). As spiritual lustre is divinely bestowed on the priest so the 'grandeur of heroism' is bestowed on the king (*ŚBr.* XIII.1.9,1f.).

The *Atharvaveda* can be said to be 'all things to all men', since it caters for all classes, from the poorest villager and agriculturist to the priests, nobility and the king. For the last it contains everything necessary for his election, inauguration, consecration, success, prosperity and protection, as well as for the welfare of his country. The high status of kings and the glory and power believed to adhere to them account for the notion of rulership as a divine right, not only in India but also in Sumeria, Egypt, and in Europe up to the eighteenth century. A fragmentary text inscribed on a Sumerian tablet from Nippur (c. twenty-third century BC) reads: 'Then kingship descended from heaven';[1] the Semitic kings boasted 'that their titles to the throne came direct from Deity and . . . not . . . through secular descent, even if they possessed royal birth'.[2]

The king as the embodiment of leadership, courage, military skill, and the distributor of booty, was regarded as the earthly counterpart of Indra, the divine war-lord and invincible conqueror. The ancient Hebrews believed their kings were imbued with Yahweh's power, thus his spirit 'came mightily upon David' from the day he was anointed king (1 Sam. 16:13), and hence the Hebrew monarchs were regarded as an extension of the divine personality.

The king was entitled to the whole-hearted support of his warriors, as they were to that of their individual bands of fighting men. This 'feudal' system was not unlike that adopted by the Norman and Angevin kings, who relied on their barons, as did their knights on their men-at-arms when at war. In peacetime the roles of priest and ruler were complementary, but perhaps to ensure that they remained so, the priests insisted that the king – who was usually illiterate – should have a literate priestly adviser (*purohita*) who, according to the later law books, should be a master of atharvanic lore. Furthermore, they insisted that no ruler should attempt to rule without appointing a *purohita*; if he did so his efforts to govern would fail and his sacrificial offerings would be useless (*Aitareya Brāhmaṇa* VIII.24). Thus it appears that the *purohita* represented the real power of the king.

The *purohita* was usually a gifted man, a good organizer, a master of the mantras and incantations necessary to protect the king from enemies and the intrigues of rivals, as well as causing hostile witchcraft to revert to its originators (*AV.* X.1,6). The *purohita* claimed that he was the earthly representative of Bṛhaspati, the lord of prayer and spells,[3] and *purohita* of the gods (*Aitareya Brāhmaṇa* III.17), who gained and held for them the magical powers obtained from the sacrifice, powers which were bestowed on Bṛhaspati's earthly counterpart, who in turn shared them with his royal master. All oblations possess great power, but that of a *purohita* could increase the power and glory of the ruler (*AV.* VI.39; VI.78). The prestige of *purohitas* varied as did that of kings, as is indicated in the account of the 'War of the Ten Kings' (*daśarājña*). Shortly before it began, Viśvāmitra, the *purohita* of King Sudās, was dismissed and replaced by Vasiṣṭha. Viśvāmitra forthwith joined the ten kings opposed to Sudās, warning them that failure to combine would result in their individual defeat. Though they accepted Viśvāmitra's advice, it came too late and they were defeated. A bitter feud between the two *purohitas* ensued which was carried on by their descendants long after its origin was forgotten.

The *purohita* was mainly responsible for various ceremonies including the *rājasūya*, originally a simple rite of the consecration of a king based on *AV.* IV.8. It reminded the royal candidate that though he might become a most powerful ruler, yet the god of Death (Mṛtyu) is ever-present and must be propitiated, as must the other unknown forces which assail mankind, if a long and peaceful reign is to be achieved. Death is the archetype of justice, the requiter (*dharma-rāja*) of all deeds, both bad and good. But the ruler had to face other hazards against which it was considered necessary that his power, i.e., his 'royalty', should be renewed every morning when his *purohita* recited a prayer, and he and the king exchanged water-vessels. The king is then given an amulet of *parṇa* or *palāśa* wood (*Butea monosperma*)[4] similar to that which had once belonged to the gods who had secreted it in a *parṇa* tree. Its divine strength is transmitted to the wearer of the amulet and ensures that he will never lack the loyalty of his vassals or of his people. The god Varuṇa, the first sovereign and the embodiment of the power of sovereignty,[5] presides at the king's consecration, a ceremony which ritually reproduces the archetypal act of Varuṇa's consecration in ancient times. Among the ruler's other functions are the protection of the moral order which was thought to depend on the moral probity of the ruler, and the preservation of the magical power of the mighty (*asurasya māyā*) which controls the universe.

With the completion of the *rājasūya* ceremony the ruler was endowed with lustre and glory (qualities regarded as separate entities), which are attracted to a wise and moral king. To indicate the vastness of his domains he ritually strides towards the four cardinal points, and then steps on to a tiger-skin, a symbol of his royal status. The tiger-skin transmits to the king the power of the tiger, the king of animals.[6] The tiger-skin itself was also believed to have a re-invigorating and re-integrating effect on the ruler.[7] The *rājasūya* ritual (*Kauś.* 17,1–10) appears to relate to the earliest form of the ceremony and prescribes, not a tiger-skin, but a bull-hide, probably because of the unavailability of the former in north-western India. During the performance of this part of the ritual the *purohita* draws consecrated water from one of the sacred rivers. A bowl of cooked rice is then consecrated, and the king sprinkled with holy water, a lustration that both purified and revivified the king as it did the Pharaohs of ancient Egypt.[8] The *purohita* seats the king on the throne (symbolizing the 'world's navel' or centre of the world) placed on a bull-hide.[9] The king and priest then fill two vessels with water, one from the other, and then exchange them, the *purohita* saying: 'In common to us be the good and bad we do.' To which the king replies: 'Which of us two shall do evil, let it be his alone, but the good shall belong to us both.' The *purohita* then hands the consecrated rice to the king to eat, after which he mounts his horse and turns it towards the north-east (the invincible region), the realm of the gods and the gate of heaven (*ŚBr.* 6.6.2,4). The eating of consecrated food is particularly beneficial because it transmits to the eater the special power accruing to the sacrifice.

According to the *Ṛgvidhāna* (II.19,1ff.) a man who aspires

to kingship should bathe on a red skin; a king, on a tiger-skin; a noble on a *ruru* deer-skin; and a workman on a goat-skin.

Despite the magical rites prescribed for the protection and well-being of a ruler, he was expected to ensure that his *purohita* performed the required expiatory rites (*śānti*) in his (the ruler's) domestic-fire; as well as the rites for the prosperity of his country and people, and the sorcery (*abhicāra*) necessary to repel enemies (*Gautama Dharma Sūtra* 11.15,17). The *purohita* also had to oversee the complete arming of the king and his troops. For this a particular ritual based on *AV.* VI.98 was employed which called on Indra, the divine archetype of courage and military prowess, to watch over him. His safety when asleep was ensured, not only against the hazards of assassination, but also against the attacks of non-human malevolent forces.

The *rājasūya* ceremony (referred to above) subsequently became associated with another – the *vājapeya*, meaning 'libation of strength', and associated with the welfare of warriors (*kṣatriya*). The cup of mead offered to the hero in Valhalla by the Valkyrie may be an extension of the *vājapeya*, in that the warrior's welfare is similarly looked after in the next world, the drink being a 'highly charged and significant symbol of the passing of the hero to the realm of the gods . . . a drink giving freedom from time and immortality'.[10] The libation was drunk at one of the *soma* sacrifices performed by a king or priest aspiring to attain higher status, or at the elevation of a priest to the position of *purohita*, or that of a member of a royal family succeeding to the throne. But the *aśvamedha* (horse sacrifice) was the most complex of all the royal ceremonies and constituted the official recognition of imperial status of a king of kings (*ekarāja*), a position conceded by rivals too weak to resist, or by those who had done so and been defeated, or whose kingdoms had been annexed or reduced to the status of vassals. These ceremonies, elaborated by the priests from existing popular practices, employed mantras, charms and 'sympathetic magic', and were much favoured by priests, because of the largesse they received on these occasions. The performance of a horse-sacrifice also increased the prestige of the ruler's *purohita* who claimed to be personally responsible for much of the success achieved by the newly created emperor. So close were the ties of ruler and *purohita* that the relationship was regarded as a symbol of perfect unity (*ŚBr.* VI.6,3), but such a state could have only been possible when a high degree of Aryan and Indian co-operation had been achieved. Even then royal power was often insecure and short-lived, and hence the necessity of spells and charms to maintain the *status quo*.[11] In addition, its preservation required that the king should be healthy, wealthy, strong, courageous, and with vast stores of jewels and rich regalia for himself and the royal elephant (a symbol of royalty) which he rode on State occasions. Similarly, the ancient Egyptian Pharaoh's magnificent appearance and insignia identified him with the gods. Even his crowns were imbued with supernatural life; the uraeus on his forehead spat forth flames which consumed rebels.

The Indian royal elephant was one having an unusually light-grey hide (described as 'white'), which indicated its divine origin; it was the terrestrial counterpart of Indra's own great four-tusked white elephant, Airāvata, the rain-giver and bestower of fertility, prosperity and royal power.

The ideal ruler was worthy of his position provided he was of high moral stature, heroic and capable of protecting his people. A weak king laid the country open to attack and possible devastation. Such a result is not unlike the ancient Hebrew belief that a king's misrule reacted on the land and caused it to become barren, as exemplified by King Saul's decimation of the Gibeonites and the devastation of their land, despite a treaty of friendship. His action resulted in a famine which affected both peoples and the Hebrew theologians regarded it as a divine punishment.

Although a ruler was required to be militarily capable, 'skilled in archery . . . and a mighty chariot-fighter' (*ŚBr.*

XIII.1.9), he was also expected to be of handsome appearance and to have strength of character. Thus Indra, to whom such qualities are attributed, has the epithet Śatakratu, 'Lord of a hundred powers' (*RV.* VIII.32,11). Indra's mother, the goddess Aditi, also typifies 'boundless' strength, and hence her epithet Śavasī 'Mighty One'; his wife Śacī also symbolizes the power which was the source of his energy.

The force inherent in sacrificial oblations was derived from the gods who, by means of the *śākamedha* oblation, were able to slay the demonic Vṛtra (*ŚBr.* II.5.3,1). Offerings made to the gods actually partake of their divinity and power, which the priestly supervisor of the sacrifice can then direct towards the achievement of beneficent or maleficent ends. The ritual (*Kauś.* 13,3–6) necessary to attain kingly power and glory (both god-given attributes) is based on *AV.* VI.38;39, and directs that an amulet composed of hair from the navel of a *snātaka* (a student priest who has performed the absolution ceremony and thus completed his discipleship), and hair from a lion, tiger, goat, ram and a king, be pasted together with lac and covered with gold. To protect the king from diseases caused by demons, he wears an amulet made from splinters of ten kinds of sacred wood. The power of the trees from which the splinters are taken is transmitted to the ruler through them. Other rites prescribe that the vital organs of any of the animals mentioned in the previous rite should be mixed with rice and eaten by the king who will then share that particular animal's strength, speed, potency, etc., but to acquire longevity and the power of the elephant (*hastivarcas*), the king wears an ivory amulet (*AV.* III.22).

The Indo-Iranians personified the glory, fame and splendour attaching to great kings and heroes. These qualities remained with them until death, or departed immediately they committed an unworthy act. Thus the Iranian divinity Khvarənah (the embodiment of the above qualities) left an unworthy king in the shape of a bird.

The kingly Glory also dwelt with Zoroaster and became

associated with the Glory of Iran (Airyanam khvarənah), which enemies often attempted to seize. According to the legendary history of the first Sassanian ruler, Ardašīr Pāpakān, this Glory (in the form of a ram) left Ardabān, the last Parthian king, and ran after Ardašīr, thus indicating that the sovereignty had passed to him.[12] Similarly, Indra lost his vital power when Tvaṣṭṛ (the divine craftsman) exorcized him for having killed his (Tvaṣṭṛ's) son Viśvarūpa. Tvaṣṭṛ brought *soma*-juice suitable for 'witchery' but withheld it from Indra, who forcibly seized and drank it, thereby desecrating the sacrifice. Immediately Indra's body burst asunder and his energy or vital power flowed away from every limb (*ŚBr.* XII.7.1,1ff.). According to the *Ṛgvidhāna* (II.15,6), by worshipping fire and muttering *RV.* V.4,9–10 one 'escapes all misfortune and acquires imperishable glory'.

The *Atharvaveda* includes various ceremonies for the restoration of an exiled king. One of these ceremonies (III.3) directs that Agni (who here takes the place of Indra) be invoked to ensure that the exile's return will be as straight and swift as an eagle's flight, that the twin Aśvins will remove all obstacles from his path; and that his people and Indra will support him and help to scatter his enemies. Brahmaṇaspati (the lord of prayer) is invoked (*AV.* I.29), to bestow on the exiled king the magical wheel-shaped amulet, like that worn by Indra to increase his power, the wheel being a symbol of the *cakravartin* (universal ruler), and indicating his unimpeded progress throughout his dominions. This notion is confirmed by the ritual (*Kauś.* 16,29) which directs that the amulet be made from part of the rim of an actual chariot wheel. Thus, as the wheels of the invincible sun's chariot move across the heavens, so shall the king's armies invincibly advance on earth. The above ritual – with some variations – is also included in the *rājasūya*, the annual consecration of a king as a ceremony of cosmic regeneration.

Another rite for the restoration of a king prescribes that a rice-cake shaped like a couch [or throne][13] be placed on *darbha* grass and submerged in water; a piece of earth from his former kingdom is spread over the hearth, and the king is then served with a bowl of porridge and milk. Four days later he receives a rice-cake which he eats. Then he is recalled to his kingdom.

During the Vedic era, many of the smaller kingdoms were often subject to the ambitions of powerful rulers, but gradually the notion of an ideal ruler and an ideal state developed from which was derived the conception of the 'world ruler', the saviour of the world, envisaged as Kalkin, the future incarnation (*avatāra*) of the Supreme Being Viṣṇu, who will one day appear, mounted on a white horse, and bearing a blazing sword. His mission will be to bring peace and justice to the world, as will Maitreya the future Buddha; or the 'holy Prince' of the Greek Sibyllene oracles; or the Zervanite fiery horseman whose appearance in the sky will coincide with the end of the world; or the Christ of the Apocalypse.

FIVE

Battle charms

Little is known of the relationship that existed among the various cultures of northern India prior to the arrival of the Aryans. The brief allusions to this period in the *Ṛgveda* and the *Atharvaveda* reveal only the existence of some of the Indus valley city states, on whose welfare the indigenous tribes of the immediate hinterland depended for their livelihood. But the arrival of the Aryans, with their different social structure and patriarchal religion, resulted in resistance by guerrilla groups of the indigenes, culminating in organized warfare as the Aryans spread eastwards.

The elephants and weapons of the indigenes were generally no match for the more mobile horse-drawn chariots of the Aryans, but both sides made use of battle charms (*saṁgrāmikāṇi*)[1] which they regarded as efficacious as their weapons. The battle charms were of two kinds, called *apanodanāni* and *mohanāni*.[2] The purpose of the first was for driving away (*apanodana*) the enemy, the second to deceive and confuse him by all possible means. Descriptions of the weapons are generally explicit, the most important of them being the bow and arrow. It was used as it still is, by drawing the bow-string back to the ear, and hence the arrow is called *karṇayoni* (originating from the ear) (*RV*. II.24,8); the twang of the bow-string was likened to the whisper of a beloved woman. The last act of the funeral rite was the removal of the bow from the dead warrior's hand, in the hope that it would transmit the might and glory of the dead warrior to his successors (*RV.* X.18,9).

Poisoned arrows were used in Vedic warfare (but later were forbidden by law), and hence the necessity for charms to counteract the poison. Some Aryan warriors were equipped with spears and lances, but a *vajra* (the so-called thunderbolt) was the favourite weapon of Indra, the Aryan war-god. The sharp-edged discus (*cakra*)[3] was also used and later became Viṣṇu's emblem, which was personified as Sudarśana. The latter was believed to incorporate part of the deity, thus becoming the centre of a separate cult. Traps, snares and nets were used in war; old ropes were burned to produce thick smoke and a nauseating smell; the thunderous sounds of the battle-drum (*dundubhi*; *ānaka*) both rallied the Aryan warriors and endowed them with vigour, but struck terror into the enemy (*AV.* V.20, etc.). The *bakura*, a kind of horn or wind instrument, was also used to rally troops in battle.[4]

The personification of weapons (*āyudhapuruṣa*) was a common practice in India as among the Sumerians, Babylonians and Canaanites. The Hebrews applied the term *messiah* not only to their great religious leaders but also to their shields, implying that they also possessed sacred power; similarly the Shoshone Indians of North America believed their shields possessed supernatural powers which made them impenetrable. In Europe there were many personified weapons including Miölnir, Thor's hammer; Excalibur, King Arthur's sword; the Irish sword Caladbolg of Fergus; to all of which were ascribed magical powers. The Celts personified their weapons and worshipped them as well as ascribing magic powers to the weapons of gods and heroes.

The wooden battle-drum, equipped with the skin of a cow, is personified and addressed (*AV.* V.20 and 21) and likened to a warrior sure of victory. Its sound terrifies the enemy, ensures booty;[5] and is possessed by all the *gotras*.[6] The drum is carried before the army (as was also customary in European warfare) and is called the 'fist of Indra' (*RV.* VI.47,29ff.).

Today in Nigeria and other parts of Africa, certain drums are regarded as sacred and kept in special shrines. Offerings of food and oil are made to them.

Before battle all musical instruments are ritually washed in a mixture containing certain fragrant substances and then anointed with dregs of ghee. Finally the *purohita*, the king's priest and adviser on sacred and secular matters, sounds each instrument thrice – probably as a kind of consecration – before handing them back to the warriors. As a further stimulus, the warriors took part in a pre-battle dance like the war-dances of Ancient Egyptian, African and American-Indian tribes. Indra is said to enact his heroic exploits in dance (*RV.* V.33,6), which may mean that battle itself was regarded as a war-dance as in Old German poetry and in Homer's Epics. Banners were carried in the van of the army and served to rally the warriors.[7] The armies appear to have been composed of foot-soldiers – supported by charioteers, each with a warrior who stood on the charioteer's left. Cavalry was unknown in Vedic times, but chariot horses were greatly valued in war; Indra's bay horses are frequently mentioned, probably because bays were favoured by the Aryans. According to Ridgeway,[8] the Vedic horses were of Mongolian stock; the so-called Tangum horses from the Tangustan Mountains of Bhotan had white legs and large areas of bay on the body. But it is just possible that the Vedic horses were the Caspian miniature horses – the ceremonial horses of ancient Persia which were recently 'discovered' in 1965 in Iran. Before that they were thought to have been extinct for over a thousand years. The Mesopotamians also used the Caspian in the third millennium BC, and also the Sasanians from the fifth century BC to the seventh AD. By 1977 about thirty-five Caspians have been bred in the UK.

One *RV. sūkta* (IV.38) is dedicated to Dadhikras, probably the name of a famous chariot horse; another *sūkta* (VI.75), addressed to war-weapons, also praises the mailed warrior and the skilful charioteer whose horses' hoofs trample on the enemy. The war-chariot itself was personified and oblations made to it by the warrior. The above *sūkta* is also employed to consecrate the various parts of the chariot and its horses; a consecration which ensures victory (*Ṛgvidhāna* II.24,3ff.).

The use of special mantras and oblations called *rāṣṭrabhṛts* (*rāṣṭra* 'kingdom', *bhṛt* 'bearing sway') are also necessary to support the kingdom. When the gods and Asuras were in conflict, Indra had recourse to Prajāpati for aid, and the latter gave him the *rāṣṭrabhṛts* which ensure strength and victory and hence were called 'victorious'. An exiled ruler should have these oblations offered for him that he may regain his kingdom. They are also offered at the commencement of battle for they represent the kingdom and those who strive to retain it (*Tait. Saṁ.* iii.4,6). But to bring a king, country or fortified town into subjection, an offering of one's own blood should be made (*Ṛgvidhāna* III.18,3f.).

Originally the Vedic warriors' chief incentive was the need to protect the community, or alternatively the desire for booty, usually cattle. In several passages of the *RV.* (I.91,23; III.47,4, etc.) the term for warfare was *gaviṣṭi* (literally 'desire for cows'). The battle charms used for these forays were naturally associated with Indra the Aryan war-god, called the 'son of strength', also with the god of fire Agni, who in this context ignites the scrub or forest and so cuts off the retreat of the enemy. Among early peoples much ritual was attached to the preparation and the going to war, which was never commenced until all omens were favourable, thus *AV.* I.19 was used to counteract any evil portents. When once the auspicious day was fixed, it was usually followed by a week of elaborate rites, and on the eve of battle the king harangued his troops and afterwards feasted them. That night he slept in his chariot within reach of his armour and weapons. Before dawn his personal priest armed him with his breastplate, simultaneously reciting a charm to ensure the ruler's protection from death, praying that the same defensive methods used by the gods of old when fighting for sovereignty should also aid the king (*AV.* XIX.20).

Before leading his army into battle a fire is lit and fed with rotting rope, and prodded with two sticks of *aśvattha* and *vadhaka* wood – both woods being associated with magical rites for the destruction of enemies. An oblation of *iṅgiḍa* (an unknown plant or substance) and butter is put on a fire of *vadhaka* wood, using the inauspicious left hand. A branch of red *aśvattha* is then fixed in the ground on the north side of the fire and a red and blue thread (the colours of hostile sorcery) wound round it. After a brief interval the *aśvattha* branch is removed and fixed to the south of the fire, the region of death, thus symbolizing the death of the enemy.

Sometimes Soma, the Maruts, Mitra and Varuṇa and the *soma*-drinking Indra are invoked for aid (*AV.* I.20), the last going before his followers fearless as a bull. Indra's favourite weapon was the metal *vajra* with a hundred or a thousand joints or edges (*RV.* I.80,6; VIII.66, etc.), which destroys both enemies and witchcraft (*AV.* VIII.5,15). Indra's courage was greatly increased by drinking the sacred *soma* juice. Whatever plant the *soma* juice was derived from, it appears to be similar in its uses and effects to the *haoma* of the Iranians. Among the many suggestions advanced is that of Wasson who considers that it was the hallucinogenic fly agaric mushroom (*Amanita muscaria*). Until recently *soma* was thought to be an intoxicant, but its effects as described in the texts indicates that it was a hallucinogen rather than an intoxicant.[9] This is borne out by the *ŚBr.* (5.1.2,10) which distinguishes between *soma* and *surā* (a fermented drink), the latter being said to bring only misery, but the former light, prosperity and truth. But elsewhere in the same work (XII.7.3,12) *surā* and *soma* are distilled together 'for joy' (i.e., intoxication). To joy 'the *soma*-juice contributes, and to joy also does the *surā* liquor; he thus secures both the joy of the *soma* and the joy of the *surā*: – "with the pure juice, O god, satiate the deities!"'

Indra experienced wild exhilaration, excitement and

increased power after drinking *soma* which assisted him in destroying his attackers (*RV.* VIII.12,1); the obscure verse 12 may mean that *soma* had a 'mind-expanding' effect like the modern drug LSD. *Soma* emboldened the warrior and worked him up into a battle-fury thus making him a terrifying enemy, but to the sage and poet it brought an intensity of feeling, and complete possession by the godhead, as well as the acquisition of mantic powers. The fly-agaric is regularly used by Siberian shamans and others including the Koryak, Chukchi, Yakut and Samoyed tribes, and produces ecstatic states, visions, hallucinations and delirium.

Soma, like *haoma*, was personified as a deity, and both were invoked for strength, victory, health and ecstasy. It is still customary for Zoroastrians to worship *haoma* to ensure the defeat of enemies. The drinking of stimulants by warriors during the Vedic age seems most probable; it is known that horses were given draughts of wine before battle.[10]

The *Ṛgvidhāna* (I.18,1) states that the *RV. sūkta* (I.32), glorifying Indra's deeds against seemingly overwhelming odds, was 'seen' by the sage Hiraṇyastūpa, and it should be muttered to drive back enemies. The last stanza states that Indra is the sovereign of men, king of the animate and the inanimate creations, and thus the human ruler hopes to emulate his celestial counterpart.

Among the many tactical devices employed in warfare was the 'handless shaft', which the worshippers besought the gods to cast at the enemy (*AV.* VI.65; 66; 67). Whitney suggests that it was the oblation itself, regarded as inherently powerful, but possibly it was some kind of weapon like the *cakra* which was thrown, especially as Indra is invoked to make the enemy 'collide with the great weapon' and so render them 'handless', i.e., powerless. According to a victory rite (*Kauś.* 14,7) the enemies are to be made 'handless', so causing their arms 'to shrink'. Another magical means of defeating enemies was to shake a winnowing basket containing twenty-one pebbles in their direction. This curious action is similar to that performed centuries later by Mohammed in the course of one of his many raids and battles. During most of the fighting he had remained in a hut in the rear 'praying with anxious fervour. At one point he emerged and flung a handful of pebbles in the enemy's direction, crying out: "Evil look on their faces!" He followed up this ritual gesture with religious exhortations.'[11] The Danish historian and poet Saxo Grammaticus (twelfth century) relates that the Lapps (who were noted sorcerers) escaped from their enemies by throwing three pebbles behind them which appeared as hills to their pursuers.[12] Another rite was to place rice-chaff on porridge, or a portion of small grain, as a sacrificial offering. The worthless chaff and grain indicated the warrior's low opinion of the enemy. According to the priests a king who performed a perfect sacrifice[13] was certain to be victorious.

To gain a victory the two battle-demons Arbudi and Nyarbudi, the companions of Indra, are invoked (*AV.* XI.9). To them were attributed magical powers of illusion (*māyā*) by which they confronted the enemy with terrifying apparitions and phantom armies. Arbudi is also urged to distract the enemy with hosts of celestial nymphs (*apsarasas*) accompanied by their dogs, or by demonic beings capable of assuming theriomorphic and anthropomorphic forms, the latter usually of a deformed nature. Similar apparitions sometimes appear as the spirits of ancestors when offerings are being made during funerary rites. The conjuring up of phantoms was common to many cultures including the ancient Egyptian and the Hebrew (Gen. 32:1f.). Phantoms also were associated with the Hellenic Hecate, the great goddess of ghosts and black magic; with the Teutonic Wotan, and with one of the eponymous goddesses of Ireland called Ériu who formed an army from sods of earth. The Syriac work, *Paradise of the Fathers*,[14] refers to the devils sent to tempt St Anthony: 'Now it is very easy for the Enemy to create apparitions and appearances of such a character that they shall be deemed real and actual objects. . . .'

Bṛhaspati, the lord of prayer and spells and *purohita* of the gods, represented divine power and therefore was often invoked to ensure a victorious campaign. He is all-powerful because of the power of prayer – a notion common also to ancient Egypt. It derived from an unshakeable faith in the creative power of sound (cf. the Christian Logos). It was by Bṛhaspati's aid that the gods conquered heaven and earth. Bṛhaspati envelops the enemy in the hostile colours of blue and red; colours which Kṛtyā, the goddess of witchcraft, employs to envelop her victims (*AV.* VIII.8).[15] Hostile sorcery is also carried out in a blue and red vessel (*AV.* IV.17,4), probably because these colours were originally associated with the fearsome god Rudra (*Tait. Saṁ.* IV.5.10,1), and later with Śiva (*Saura Purāṇa*).

AV. XI.9–10 are employed in victory rites. The *purohita*, after exhorting the warriors to battle, hands a bow to a warrior and lays snares, traps, etc. (perhaps miniature ones) in the expected path of the enemy, thus symbolically acting out their defeat.[16] A white-footed cow anointed with dregs of ghee is attached to the king's staff with a rope of sacred *darbha* grass called the 'flawless refuge of the gods' (*RV.* II.3,8). The grass itself was said to possess the power to split the heads of enemies (*AV.* XIX.28f.). Another white-footed cow is driven towards the enemy lines and may represent the white 'four-footed one' (perhaps symbolizing an arrow) which is said to fall on the enemy (*AV.* XI.10,20); or it may refer to driving an animal towards the enemy with lighted materials attached to their horns, as the Biblical Samson drove three hundred foxes with lighted firebrands attached to their tails, through the standing corn and olive groves of the Philistines (Judg. 15:4ff.).

Apart from the belief in the efficacy of charms and rites, no distinction appears to have been made between the efficiency of actual and mythical weapons. Homage was paid to the weapons of death (personified as Mṛtyu), and to those of gods, kings and warriors, in an attempt to propitiate them and so gain their aid (*AV.* VI.13). Lest the warrior should slacken his efforts, Manyu, the personification of the fury of battle and violent wrath, was invoked to intensify his zeal so that it shall burn (*tapas*)[17] fiercely against the enemy (*AV.* VII.93). Wrath was regarded as an independent power and identified with Indra, the heroic god of war. Thus Manyu was regarded as the victorious spirit of battle. The Zoroastrians also personified wrath and called it Aēšma.

A passage in the *ŚBr.* (IX.1.1,6) relates that Manyu alone remained faithful to the creator Prajāpati, when the gods deserted him. At this desertion Prajāpati wept with rage. His tears fell on Manyu and transformed him into the hundred-headed, thousand-eyed Rudra who strikes terror even into the gods themselves and hence he is invoked by warriors before battle.

SIX

Charms to protect priests and their possessions

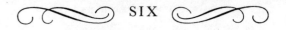

The explanation of the need for the protection of priests (*brāhmaṇas*) lies in their initial failure to obtain general recognition of their claim to special status in the community. But subsequently there was 'justification' for the claim, when they, like priests throughout the ages, were recognized as the sole mediators between gods and mankind, the inspired seers (*ṛṣis*) and recorders of divine truth and the possessors of the knowledge essential for the correct performance of sacrifices without which the cosmos would collapse, and hence they were called 'human gods'. Though their high status was generally admitted by the ruling class, the Indian indigenes naturally did not readily accept their claims, particularly their assumption of superiority because of their light-coloured skins (*ārya-varṇa*) and their highly developed language. But with the gradual fusion of the two races ethnic distinctions became less clear cut, class distinctions persisted although not firmly established until later (*RV.* X.90,12), when society became divided into four main classes: the priestly (*brāhmaṇa*), the ruling (*rājanya*), the agricultural, artisan and merchant (*vaiśya*), and finally the menial (*śūdra*). But such distinctions led ultimately to others, as in all cultures. Even in death these distinctions remained, thus it was laid down that the funeral mound of a *brāhmaṇa* should be built to the height of a standing figure; that of a ruler or warrior to the level of the arms; of a *vaiśya* to the thighs; and of a *śūdra* to the knees (*ŚBr.* XIII.8.3,11). As priestly power grew, the number of priests required for sacrificial performances increased from four to sixteen. In addition, a special office, that of religious and political adviser (*purohita*) to the king, was created. The adviser was usually a priest skilled in atharvanic lore. Many responsibilities devolved on the priests; and though some were rapacious and lax in their duties, the efforts of the majority greatly contributed to the future culture of India.

In the early days the invading Aryans were exposed to the hostility of the indigenes who, apart from using charms and sorcery against them, also attacked them and forcibly disrupted their sacrifices, desecrated the sacrificial areas and stole the priests' cattle.

The priests had no other income apart from the donations or gifts (*dakṣiṇā*)[1] (equivalent to the Zoroastrian *ašodād*) given them by the institutors of the sacrifices. The donations were an essential part of every ceremony and were believed to strengthen and ensure a perfect sacrificial performance as well as increasing the merits deriving from the sacrifice.[2] Though no fixed 'fee' was demanded, a 'donation' – according to the sacrificer's means – was expected. This was usually forthcoming, probably because of the fear of the power of the priests and their terrifying curses, as dreaded as was papal excommunication in medieval Europe. The *RV. sūkta* X.117 is 'a text in praise of gifts of wealth and food' (*dhanānnadānapraśaṃsā*), which extols the liberal man and promises that his wealth will never desert him, and condemns the miser never to be shown favour or compassion.

Great power was attributed to the *dakṣiṇā*; it was capable of shielding the donor, even against the wrath of a god. The *Taittirīya Brāhmaṇa* (II.2.5,1) relates that when some sacrificers failed to placate Varuṇa, they hid behind their respective sacrificial gifts and hence he was unable to harm them. The giving of the *dakṣiṇā* was treated as an independent sacramental act which added considerably to its awesome and mystical nature. The 'gift' was related to the desired purpose of the sacrificer, thus lame cattle were prescribed for a rite intended to injure enemies. A priest was forbidden to accept a *dakṣiṇā* previously refused by another priest, lest its inherent power should destroy him (*ŚBr.* III.5.1,25).

Some atharvanic magic formulas are intended to conjure up liberality and to exorcize avarice. The latter is personified as the lovely, golden-complexioned goddess Arāti who denotes the attraction of amassing wealth. To the niggardly she appears in erotic dreams as a naked woman who attaches herself to men. In this context she is similar to the nightmare[3] or incubus of the West – also the bringer of strange erotic dreams – which so disturbed the Christian monks and laymen of the Middle Ages.

The frequent references to the merits of liberality in the Vedas underlines the priests' continuous need for funds. Initially the 'fee'[4] was a cow; later it included bufalloes, kine, horses, ornaments, but not land. None the less, in the *ŚBr.* XIII.8.1,13, it included land, but not that owned by priests! Elsewhere in the same work (VII.1.1,4) the possession of land is said to be an inalienable right of the people.

Great rewards were held out to generous laymen. The *RV.* X.107 states that they will dwell in heaven; those who give horses will 'abide with the sun forever'; givers of gold will have eternal life; those who present robes will attain longevity. The *ŚBr.* IV.3.4,7 states that the four kinds of *dakṣiṇās* are: gold, a cow, cloth and a horse. The liberal never suffer harm or trouble and attain immortality.

The importance of *dakṣiṇā* is shown in the story of the boy Naciketas (*Kaṭha Upaniṣad*, I.1ff.), who suggested to his father Vājaśravasa that he should be given as *dakṣiṇā* so as to fulfil his father's vow to give *all* his possessions to the priests. Three times Naciketas asked his father to whom he should be given; finally his exasperated father replied: 'To Death'. The giving of one's son was the most precious sacrifice possible, thus in the Old Testament Yahweh tested Abraham's faith by commanding him to sacrifice his son, Isaac.

Some priests played upon the people's fears and anxieties regarding unusual happenings such as the birth of twins, either human or animal, which, being outside the usual course of events, were considered bad omens, requiring elaborate rites. In the case of twin animals, they finally expiated their dual existence when given to a priest![5] Human mothers of twins, however, had to pay an expiatory 'ransom' usually based on their fathers' means. Some West African tribes similarly regard the birth of twins as anomalous and thus dangerous, but a danger which can be overcome by killing the infants at birth. The fear of twins derives from the belief that two humans cannot be born from the same womb at the same time, thus one of the babies must have a supernatural origin. Similarly, night-crowing cocks are promptly killed, so that 'they do not live to contradict the definition of a cock as a bird that crows at dawn'.[6]

Barren cows were also regarded as unnatural and hence of evil portent. Their presentation to the priests was essential as priests alone were capable of coping with the dangers associated with these animals. Similarly, priests are also able to digest dangerous foods which would kill laymen. Barren ewes were also offered to the priests, the terrestrial counterparts of the gods (*Tait. Saṁ.* I.1.1,2).[7]

According to the *ŚBr.* (IV.5.1,5), the sacrificer kills a barren cow for Mitra (the divine representative of the priesthood) and for Varuṇa (the divine representative of the nobility). Twenty-one barren cows were offered at the concluding oblation (*udayanīyā*) to Mitra, Varuṇa, the Viśvedevas and Bṛhaspati. The twenty-one cows represent the twelve months of the year, the five seasons, the three worlds – earth, atmosphere and heaven; the sun making the twenty-first and representing totality (*ŚBr.* XIII.5.4,25f; cf. XIII.6.2,16).

Perhaps the priests themselves introduced the notion of the 'unnaturalness' of barren cattle to overcome the reluctance of

Sūrya. The Sun-god, British Museum

Agni. The God of Fire, British Museum

Nāga. A snake divinity,
British Museum

Sudarśana cakra. The personification
of Viṣṇu's discus, British Museum

Brahmā. The Creator and God of Wisdom, British Museum

Celestial Female Drummer, Victoria and Albert Museum

Yama. God of Death. Brahmeśvara Temple, Bhuvaneśvara

Varuṇa. Brahmeśvara Temple, Bhuvaneśvara

A flying Gandharva. Duladeva Temple, Khajuraho

rural communities to reduce their herds to what the land could support. Even today the Masai of Africa tend to overgraze the land with herds of under-nourished cattle, which represent to them status and wealth. The danger of overgrazing in India is implicit too in the constant prayers for rain and fertility. The priests also required cows ostensibly to be sacrificed to the gods, but actually for consumption by themselves because they were socially above the mundane task of providing for their own sustenance. In Vedic times the slaughter of cows – though restricted – was not prohibited.

A late atharvanic imprecation (XII.4) threatens those who fail to present a barren cow to the priest with fearsome diseases, and the ruination of their families, and death to their cattle. Whoever deceives the priests by piercing (i.e., marking) the ears of a sterile cow, claiming it for himself, finds that his possessions gradually dwindle away. Even a servant who sweeps up the dung of the animal will be affected with various deformities that will never leave him.

By giving a cow to the priest the donor ensures both the security of his own property and the priest's, but anyone who falsely declares a barren cow to be fertile to avoid parting with it, incurs the wrath of Bhava and Sarva (who represent two of the eight elemental forms of Rudra). He also incurs the hostility of other cattle who never fail to recognize that a mortal has appropriated the share intended for the gods.

The competition was keen among the priests for these cows, which probably proved a welcome addition to their wealth, but it is laid down that even if a hundred priests beg for the cow, she must be presented only to one who knows her mystic properties. The barren cow herself desires to be claimed by the priests, and her wish reaches the gods whereupon they inform the priests who come to claim her.[8] She ensures the fulfilment of all the donor's wishes, both in this world and the next.

Many Hindus believed that a cow presented to the officiant at a funerary rite would carry the deceased over the noxious river Vaitaraṇī, the boundary between the two worlds, even as an ox led the priests from the world of the Fathers (*pitṛs*) back to the world of the living (*ŚBr.* XIII.8.4,6).[9] Sometimes the tail of the *anustaraṇī*-cow slain at the funeral sacrifice was tied to the left arm of the deceased in the belief that he would be led safely over the Vaitaraṇī. Similarly in ancient Egypt the cow-headed goddess Hathor led the dead to the next world; in Syria today animals are killed on behalf of the dead and 'go before the deceased as light, to serve him in the next life as he approaches God, becoming a *kaffârah* for his sins'.[10] In northern Europe it was thought that the donor of a cow to the poor would, after death, be guided to heaven by the same animal. In Lancashire the Milky Way was called the 'cow's lane' – the way by which the dead enter heaven.[11] It seems that whichever domestic animal was most useful in different cultures was utilized as a guide for the dead, thus the spirits of the American Indians were guided over the waters of death by dogs, usually reddish ones.

The most feared of all cows was the mysterious Viliptī, created by the gods from all the barren cows offered to them. The ancient mythical seer Nārada is said to have chosen the Viliptī for himself, but its significance is not known. Bloomfield[12] suggests that it may mean '"miscarrying", a derivative of *vilupta*, "destroyed", the neuter form meaning "dead offspring" thus indicating a barren cow'. Monier-Williams (*Sanskrit–English Dictionary*) states that it refers to a cow in a particular period after calving, perhaps indicating that at a particular time it was regarded as holy and thus especially awesome and dangerous; or it may refer to a cow that has been consecrated – as *vilipta* also means 'smeared over', or 'anointed'; or perhaps it personifies barrenness. Another possibility is that it may be identical with the red cow connected with witchcraft. The *Tait. Saṁ.* (VI.4,8; VII.1,6), referring to the Viliptī cow, states that the gods, with the help of Varuṇa, decided to slay King Soma. But Soma found one thousand cows and saw among them one that contained the concentrated strength of all of them, whereupon he told Indra that he would have that one and Indra could have the rest, but the other gods each wanted a portion of the wonderful animal. They put her into the waters saying: 'Come out for Soma', whereupon she emerged in the shape of a red-brown cow of one year old, together with thirty-three others. As the price of the sacrificial *soma* was a cow, the above passages obviously have some ritual relevance.

Bṛhaspati, the divine *purohita* of the gods, rides the omniform cow Viśvarūpa (*RV.* I.161,6). Bṛhaspati enquired of the Sage Nārada the number of barren cows born among men, and which of them a non-*brāhmaṇa*, desiring prosperity, should not eat. Nārada replied that the prohibited cows included the Viliptī, and a cow that has produced a barren cow and the barren cow herself, which further supports the belief that these animals were 'rightfully' destined only for priests.

A man called Bheda (probably the leader of a non-Aryan tribe), having refused to present Indra with a barren cow, was subsquently ruined by the gods who 'talked about' him (this may mean that they cast a spell on him) and so destroyed him (*AV.* XII.4,49). Even those who merely advise against the presentation of such an animal enrage Indra, or are killed by Rudra's 'hurled missile', and one who cooks a barren cow for himself incurs the anger of all gods and priests; therefore, only an evil person, who is already ruined, would dare to eat the prohibited animal, which automatically gains magical properties merely by being in the possession of a priest. The powerful family of the Vaitahavyas once devoured a brahman's cow which resulted in all the members of the family being ruined; even the slaughtered cow avenged herself on them (*AV.* V.18 and 19). According to the ritual (*Kauś.* 48,13ff.), a priest whose cow has been stolen and eaten should recite the above mantras over the excrement within the animal's entrails and also at a burial ground. Then he exclaims thrice: 'Slay those killers'. Whilst reciting the second mantra he hides a stone in the excrement, then rests for twelve nights observing the vows of a *brahmacārin* (religious student).[13] At the end of the period, after the sun has risen twice, the thief will be destroyed.

The cow was also closely associated with witchcraft; in one charm (*AV.* XII.5,39) she is called 'witchcraft incarnate', 'deadly poisonous', and 'terrifying'; 'her cutting up is a weapon [and] her bowels a secret charm'. In Africa excrement is also associated with witchcraft. The Mandari tribe of the southern Sudan believe that witches rub stolen objects with it as a method of harming the owner. Other African sorcerers frequently use bodily refuse in their magical rites,[14] because human and animal excrement and other bodily exuviae are thought to possess potent, but dangerous properties.

A man incurs great danger if he spits upon or attacks a priest and his whole family will perish (*AV.* V.19). He is further punished by having to devour hair in the midst of a stream of blood, a punishment meted out in the next world. Wherever the pieces of an unlawfully slaughtered priest's cow are eaten or distributed the 'lustre of the kingdom' is destroyed and no hero is born there. Killing a cow is both cruel and sacrilegious; her meat is devoid of nourishment, and to drink her milk constitutes an offence against the ancestors. If an arrogant king destroys a priest's cow, his royal power and kingdom dwindle away. Also no good comes to a kingdom where priests are scorned, nor does rain fall on it. A man who scorns a priest is threatened with the performance of death rites[15] as though he were already dead; this atharvanic imprecation was greatly feared. Similarly, in medieval Christianity priests sometimes said Mass ostensibly for the dead but naming a living person whom they intended to kill. Thus the solemn chant of *Requiem aeternam dona ei, Domine*: 'Give him eternal rest, O Lord', turned the Mass into an instrument of death. Giraldus Cambrensis (who died c. 1220) stated that some priests would sing Mass for the dead ten times against a living enemy, in the hope that he would die on the tenth day. Others 'would say Mass over a wax image of the victim placed on the altar, cursing him'.[16] In ancient India those who thwarted holy work were cursed to 'go to the seat of Yama', the ruler of the dead (*AV.* II.12,7f.); the only liquid available to a persecutor of priests would be their tears and the water in which the dead have been bathed. The former would be highly dangerous since they contain the magical powers inherent in priests; the latter would be polluted because of its contact with a corpse, and the pollution would be transmitted to the drinker.

Among the many ritual uses of the consecrated rice-porridge (*brahmaudana* or *odana*), is one to prevent harm coming to a person who had eaten forbidden food or accepted prohibited gifts (*AV.* VI.71), but the priests use this atharvanic invocation to counteract priestly greed.

The firm belief in the efficacy of atharvanic spells is reflected in a passage from the Code (or law book) of Manu (XI.33) which states that the spells of the *AV.* constitute the legitimate 'weapons' which priests may use against their enemies.

SEVEN

Charms and imprecations against demons, sorcerers and others

The insecurity, both physical and economic, of ancient peoples made them particularly conscious of the many calamities that might beset them. They, like the Vedic peoples, were surrounded by many dangers, including wild animals, poisonous snakes and insects, sudden floods, droughts, famine and the attacks of the hostile indigenes. To these hazards were added the countless demonic beings created over the ages in the fertile ghost and spirit-ridden imagination of man. Witchcraft especially was greatly feared in India, as it is in Africa today, and elaborate counter-magic was necessary. The latter had great psychological value and helped to allay some of man's fears.

Basically, there is no difference between the charms and spells of shamans, priests, magicians and hostile sorcerers, since they all claim that it is possible to influence impersonal powers by symbolic communication, by prayers, gestures, mantras and incantations. These magico-religious beliefs were common to the Sumerians, Babylonians, Egyptians, Hebrews and Christians. Exorcism is still practised in Christianity. The 1972 report of the Bishop of Exeter's commission on *Exorcism* gives the rites necessary to exorcize evil spirits both from people and from places. But both the ancient Vedic priests and some modern Christian clerics condemn magical rites when practised by others.

Like the Vedic Indians, the Babylonians had a large

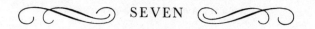

priestly class which included the *barû*, priestly seers whose function was to consult the gods and divine the future from various omens and portents; the *ašipu*, sorcerers or exorcists *par excellence* who chanted the magical texts included in the *Šurpu*, *Maqlû* and *Utukku* series; and the *zammaru*, singers of the ritual chants. Opposed to these established priests were the *kaššapu* and *kaššaptu* (the Hebrew *kaššaph*), who practised 'black magic', but it should be remembered that magic like prayer is *neutral* until directed by the agent to good or bad ends.

Vedic magic was already well established long before it began to be recorded over three thousand years ago. Many of the verses of the *Ṛgveda* (as also those of the Bible and Koran) are used for magical purposes, and the required verses for many of these rites are given in the *Ṛgvidhāna*.

A number of Indian rites are similar to those of Sumeria and Babylonia, six or seven thousand years ago,[1] and many are still used in the Near, Middle and Far East; some were adopted by the Canaanites, Hebrews, Syrians and Persians. Subsequently, they reached Europe.

Initially the charms were probably sung, later recited, and finally written down, but special powers were attributed to sung spells. Thus with one Indra revived the dead Vaikhānasas; with another he rejoined a youth's severed head to his body (*Tāṇḍya Mahābrāhmaṇa* xiv.4,7; 6,8); with the *hārāyaṇa sāman* (song or chant) he gained the power to subjugate others (xiv.9,34); and when the *ṛṣis* sought to see Indra's face it remained invisible until they sang the *nihaya sāman* (xv.5,24).[2] Sung charms (*epôdai*) were also used by the Pythagoreans to cure epilepsy and haemorrhage; traditional curing songs are still used by the Sharanahua Indians of eastern Peru, and elsewhere.

India has been pervaded with magico-religious practices since Vedic times to the modern worshippers of Śakti. They also infiltrated some of the Upaniṣads; the *Bṛhadāraṇyaka* (6.4,12) includes instructions for dealing with the lover of one's wife and directs the aggrieved husband to put fire in an unannealed vessel, and to spread out a row of reed arrows in inverse order and perform a sacrifice also in inverse order. Similar rites are also part of European black magic, the best known being the reversal of the Catholic Mass in a Black Mass. The Catholic Mass itself is a form of ceremonial magic, and achieves a magical result by the changing of ordinary bread and wine into the divine which 'the worshipper consumes . . . to become one with God'.[3] The transformation is produced by the priest's words 'of consecration'. He assumes the person of Christ for the duration of the ritual and uses the same ceremonies and actions believed to have been performed by Christ at the Last Supper,[4] without which the rite would be ineffective.

Roman Catholics, recognizing the magical powers inherent in the Mass, have used it to achieve various ends, either maleficent or beneficent. A Dominican priest in the sixteenth century tried to exorcize a demon from a child by touching her throat with a vessel full of hosts. A number of Christian prayers were also used for cursing, and included the solemn chant: *Requiem aeternam dona ei, Domine*, 'Give him eternal rest, O Lord'; the *Deus laudem* was frequently used as a slaying prayer, as were Psalms 94 and 109. The Lord's Prayer occurs in most Christian spells, but in a Black Mass it becomes 'Our Father, which *wert* in heaven. . .'.

The most sacred Hindu mantra, the *sāvitrī* or *gāyatrī* (*RV.* III.62,10) addressed to the sun, when uttered in inverted order destroys enemies and is infallible.[5] Fuel of *vibhītaka* (*Terminalia bellerica*) wood is thrown on the fire to produce obstructing influences against enemies during the whispered recitation of the *sāvitrī* (*Ṛgvidhāna* I.15,6; according to the *Atharvavedapariśiṣṭa* 26.5,3, it will also ruin enemies).

Most charms in the above category belong to the terrible (*ghora*) side of Vedic practices known as *abhicāra* and *yātuvidyā*,[6] and are traditionally associated with the semi-divine family of Aṅgiras; hence such charms are also known as *aṅgirasaḥ* which constitutes the second part of the old designation of the *Atharvaveda* – *atharvāṅgirasaḥ*. Probably some members of this family were innovators of part of the Vedic ritual by means of the performance of a particular sacrificial rite (*Tait. Saṁ.* VIII.1.4,1).

Men as well as supernatural beings may practise witchcraft and hence anyone can become a sorcerer (*RV.* V.12,2), provided the necessary training is undergone. Elsewhere in the *RV.* (VII.104,15f.), a man swears: 'May I die this day . . . if I be a demon', and lays a curse on the man who has falsely accused him. The last *sūkta* consists mostly of imprecations directed against various demons and spirits – *rākṣasas*, *yātudhānas*, *kimīdins*, and all other beings and forces believed to be inimical to man. Soma is urged to throw them to the serpent, or consign them to the 'lap of Nirṛti' (i.e., destruction). The demoness (*rākṣasī*), who wanders about at night as silently as an owl, is commanded to fall into a deep cavern or be crushed by the press-stones (*adri*) used in the *soma* sacrifice. She resembles the 'night-monster' of Isaiah (34:14), the Lilith of Rabbinical tradition.

The powerful oblation (always associated with Agni as the oblation-bearer to the gods) is called upon to gather up sorcerers and carry them, as a river carries foam, to the place of sacrifice where they will be recognized and dealt with. Oblations offered to divinities become consecrated through the performance of the sacrifice, thus a person partaking of the oblations gains something of the gods' 'divineness'.

Lead amulets are specially efficacious against demons (*AV.* I.16; *Kauś.* 47,23); lead is also employed ritually in witchcraft to kill enemies and the hordes of demonic beings who prowl about during the night of the full moon. Indra is said to have given lead to man for the express purpose of dispelling all kinds of demons. If a cow or servant is killed by fiends they must be pierced with lead. If the murderer is a man, ground lead should be put in his food, or on his personal ornaments; he is then struck with a decayed bamboo-reed staff, the length of an arm. Later the opposite view was held in Europe that demons were invulnerable to lead bullets but vulnerable to those of silver. None the less, Christian churches often used leaden caskets to protect religious relics from demonic attacks and also to preserve the virtue believed to be inherent in relics.

The *ŚBr.* (V.4.1,9f.) equates lead with the head of the demon Namuci which Indra tore off. From it a *rākṣasa* arose saying: 'Where are you going? Where will you rid yourself of me?' This reflects the belief that guilt itself was an entity which actually adhered to the perpetrator of a crime. Thus when Śiva cut off one of Brahmā's heads it stuck fast to his hand until he had expiated the crime. Indra finally succeeded in beating off Namuci with a disk of lead, since when lead became soft.[7] Lead is also used to exorcize the demonic Agni Kravyad, the flesh-devouring funerary fire.

Another charm (*AV.* I.28) is used ritually for relief from fear of witches (*Kauś.* 26,26). Here again Agni is urged to 'burn away' deceivers, sorcerers, *kimīdins*, and to force the *yātudhānī* (witch) to eat her own children. Witches are described as having 'horrible hairs' which may indicate their association with the sinister long-haired 'evil-wailers' mentioned elsewhere in the *AV.* The Bhils of Central India tortured suspected witches and then cut off a lock of their hair and buried it, so breaking the last link of their magical powers. Europeans also believed that the maleficent powers of witches resided in their hair, and thus they could not be harmed until every hair on their bodies was shaved off, and hence many witches were shaved before being burnt alive.[8]

An important class of spells used in exorcism is called *cātanāni* (expellers), and attributed to the *ṛṣi* Cātana whose name means 'driving away'. One of this class is *AV.* I.7.

The effects of curses were greatly feared in ancient cultures as in parts of the world today. Basically a curse and a blessing are the same, because a spell pronounced by a holy person and containing a divine name or names may draw down prosperity or adversity according to the intention of the agent. This is borne out by the Bible story which relates that Moses, because of his close connexion with Yahweh, possessed a special power of blessing and cursing as did Hebrew priests after him. Blessings and curses are said to lie on the two sacred mountains enclosing the valley of Shechem, ready to descend with rewards or punishments as circumstances require (Deut. 11:29). The Psalms were greatly favoured for cursing, the Psalter being regarded as a sure defence against demons, but to ensure that an evil man received his full punishment it was always necessary to curse him.

To counteract the effects of curses an unspecified plant was made into an amulet (*AV.* II.7). This 'curse-effacing plant' wiped away the curses of rivals, relatives and priests as easily as water washes away dirt. Its root stretches down from the sky, and protects offspring, wealth, and counteracts hostile witchcraft, the effects of the Evil Eye,[9] and the evil intentions of enemies. Furthermore, it causes curses to recoil on their instigators. This belief is also common among the Yorubas of Nigeria who still undertake elaborate rites to make curses revert to their initiators.[10]

To prevent a man being possessed by the demon Grāhi (Seizer) an amulet is worn made from the splinters of ten different trees (*AV.* II.9). The Babylonian demon Aḫḫazu also 'seized' men, as did the demonic beings who emerged from the underworld. This tradition gradually reached the Arabs and gave rise to the belief in Jinns – supernatural beings combining beneficent and maleficent powers. A *sraktya* amulet counteracts witchcraft and acts like a powerful weapon (*AV.* VIII.5), and causes sorcery to recoil on its instigator. This type of defensive charm is characterized by the word *prati* and its derivatives and compounds; thus *prativāra* means 'warding off'; *pratīpa* 'against the stream', 'hindering', equivalent to the English 'going against the grain'; *pratiharaṇa*, 'repelling', 'throwing back'; *pratihāra* a magical spell recited over weapons; *prativiṣa* 'antidote' (i.e.

counter-poison). In olden times Indra, with a *sraktya* amulet, slew Vṛtra, conquered the anti-gods (Asuras), the Heavens and the whole world. Thus the power of this amulet is increased by its divine association with Indra and with the great sage Kaśyapa.

A spell directed against those who would thwart another's incantations is called 'Bharadvāja's cleaver' (*bharadvājapravraskam*), the ancient *ṛṣi* Bharadvāja being its reputed innovator (*AV.* II.12). It accompanies the ritual cutting of wood to make a staff, a necessary adjunct of witchcraft rites, and one of the supreme emblems of magical power.[11] A number of divinities, including Heaven and Earth, the mistress of the field (*kṣetrasya patnī*) who is the guardian of cultivated land, and the solar Viṣṇu, are invoked that they may be 'inflamed' against those whom the petitioner hates.[12] Heaven and Earth were also frequently invoked in Babylonian exorcizing charms. To overcome the power of evil it is essential to have some divine authority as a support. The simplest method is to use the name of a divine being or thing, the inherent potency of the names being thought to increase the efficacy of the rite. From Vedic times word-magic was a regular feature of sacrificial ritual. One method was to recite the names of the ancient *ṛṣis* because, having themselves already obtained the innumerable merits deriving from the sacrifice, their very names would ensure the effectiveness of the suppliant's sacrifice.[13] Those who would harm the petitioner shall be 'fettered' (afflicted) by disease; those who think themselves superior to him, or who revile his incantations, shall find that their own wrong-doings will 'burn' them. Here heat (*tapas*) is used as a weapon against evil-doers. Similarly Agni-rakṣohan 'the killer of *rakṣas* (demons)' is urged to burn enemies (*RV.* IV.4,4). 'Agonies of burning' are said to be the portion of wrongdoers (*RV.* VI.52,2); a notion reminiscent of descriptions of the Christian hell, but the Vedic punishments are not eternal. The enemy is led by Agni Kravyad (the funerary fire) to Yama's seat (i.e., to death).[14] The ritual

(*Kauś*. 47,25–9) prescribes that *AV*. II.12 be recited whilst one of the footprints of an enemy running in a southerly direction (the sphere of the dead) is cut with a leaf from a *paraśu* tree, or with the blade of an axe (*paraśu* means both 'tree' and 'axe'). Along the length of the footprint three lines are cut and three across, the dust is removed from the footprint and tied up in a *palāśa* (*Butea monosperma*) leaf and then thrown into a fire-pan. If the dust crackles it signifies that the enemy has been overthrown. The footprints and the shadow of a man or animal were regarded as actual parts of the beings themselves, thus a man can be killed by stabbing his shadow, or burnt by burning dust from his footprint. In Hinduism, dust from the hoof-marks of a cow (a particularly auspicious animal) was used to drive away demons from the infant Kṛṣṇa. In Africa the use of dust in spells has a modern magical application. A Nigerian lorry driver quarrelled with a man who later collected some sand and earth marked by the tyre treads of the lorry. From them a magical medicine was prepared, and shortly afterwards the driver was killed in an accident![15]

To defeat rivals, witches, *piśācas* and *sadānvās* the ritual (*Kauś*. 48,1) uses *AV*. II.18 in a witchcraft rite performed whilst adding reeds to a fire. This somewhat resembles the instructions on the Mesopotamian Ritual Tablet I (belonging to the magical series called *Šurpu*) and also in some ancient Egyptian magical books such as the *Harris Magical Papyrus* and the *Salt Magical Papyrus*, which all direct that the ritual be accompanied by particular prayers or charms as in Vedic ritual. When performing the ritual for the *Šurpu* series, the priest places reeds crosswise on a brazier around which is sprinkled a circle of flour,[16] so separating and shutting out pollution from the sacrificial area. It was also customary to make shallow furrows round Vedic altars; the Parsees similarly mark out ritual objects; and the Mandaeans of Iraq and Iran demarcate the sacrificial area.

Particular plants are frequently used in Vedic and Semitic

magic, 'whenever evil sorcery besets a man'.[17] The *apāmārga* plant repels curses, as well as the sorcery prepared by enemies in an unannealed vessel (*AV.* IV.17). The latter is one which has not been toughened by heat to remove its brittleness by the process of annealing. Thus it indicates the disintegrating effects of witchcraft on the victim. (The vessel represents the victim as in Haitian Voodoo.) The *apāmārga* has the capacity to 'wipe off' disease, curses, barrenness and even bad luck at dice – a notion derived from its supposed etymology, *apa marj* (to wipe out). The same notion also occurs in the Mesopotamian *Šurpu* series of magical rites in which sickness, curses, errors and crimes are 'wiped out' by the priest.[18] The Greeks also believed that guilt was something external to man and which clung to him. Furthermore, it could spread from one person to another like an infectious disease, thus it had to be quickly 'wiped off' with water, or violently effaced by fire, or absorbed by wool, fleece, eggs or other objects.[19]

The personification of witchcraft is Kṛtyā – a word which has a number of meanings including: an evil spell or charm, a doll-like effigy; a magical performance; and a maleficent spirit. The *apāmārga* plant and the stars and sun are called upon to nullify the effects of witchcraft (*AV.* IV.18). Whoever makes an evil charm (*kṛtyā*) and secretes it in a person's house without his knowledge, that spell will revert to the instigator and fasten on him like a suckling calf to a cow. Many attempts have been made to explain verse three of the above charm which states that whoever makes evil at home seeking to cause the death of another, the act will be accompanied by a loud crash when the *kṛtyā* is burned. The feminine 'it' refers to the *kṛtyā*[20] and may mean that when witchcraft is being performed, counter-magic will destroy the *kṛtyā* by burning and by stones crashing down on it;[21] or it may mean that the charm is burnt on stones and their cracking indicates that the victim has been destroyed.

The *Ṛgvidhāna* (II.9,3) states that a *kṛtyā* may be conjured up from water by means of a hundred thousand 'ash-oblations';[22] in the *Mahābhārata* Vṛṣādarbhi produced from the fire a *kṛtyā* whom he called a *yātudhānī*.

The first charm of Book X of the *AV.* also belongs to the sorcery-repelling class (*kṛtyāpratiharaṇāni*) and refers to a *kṛtyā* hand-made by adepts. To counteract such witchcraft the Āṅgirasa (the appointed priest or *purohita*) turns the spells in the opposite direction, and slays their senders; he sends the sorcerer's spell 'against the current, up-stream', thus proving his power to be superior.[23] A *kṛtyā* can be hidden in various places, including the grassy seat (*barhis*) prepared for the gods at sacrifices, or in fields, burial grounds or a householder's domestic hearth.

Although there are frequent references to the continual struggles between the gods and the anti-gods, both originated from the creator Prajāpati. (Similarly, in the Old Testament, good and evil spirits were created by Yahweh.) In ancient times the anti-gods used *kṛtyās* in an attempt to defeat the gods, but the latter dug 'sounding holes' of arm's length and found the magically charged objects which they dug up, so rendering them harmless (*ŚBr.* III.5.4,1–14; see also *Tait. Saṁ.* VI.2,11). Magically potent objects like bones, nails, hair, dust from the intended victim's footprint, or other objects could be used in hostile rites. Whichever object was chosen was tied up in a worn piece of cloth and buried. In many cultures the outer parts of the body were regarded as inauspicious and hence dangerous. Thus if a woman was the intended victim, a lock of her hair, nail-parings or inauspicious personal objects were crushed by three stones in a mortar before being buried.

There are similarities between the *kṛtyā* and the present-day Haitian Voodoo *wanga*, defined by Métraux as 'a term which is applied to any object or objects which has received, as a result of magic procedure, a property that is harmful to one or more people. *Wangas* are also called "poisons" . . . [but] these concoctions are only poisonous on the supernatural plane. . . In Haiti the power of a *wanga* is often personified.'[24] Its efficacy is then attributed to a spirit (like the Vedic Kṛtyā) which has been invested in the now magically potent object.

AV. V.31 refers to a number of animate and inanimate things in which *kṛtyās* may be placed. They include a 'raw' (unannealed) vessel, mixed grains, raw flesh, a cock, a horned goat, ewe, a one-hoofed animal, animals with teeth in both jaws; cattle, donkey, rootless [plant], a house, assembly hall (*sabha*), gambling-board, dice, arrow, drum, well, seat, human bone, etc. The last verse calls upon Indra to slay with his deadly weapon, the witch, those who conceal spells, and the possessors of roots by means of which much sorcery was carried out. The ritual designates the above objects as *marmāṇi* 'vital spots'. *Marman* means a vulnerable point, any exposed or sensitive part of the body, or vital organ. According to the *Nirukta* there are 107 such points. This notion was based on the belief that a man is as vulnerable through his belongings as in his own person. Thus he may be killed by merely stabbing his shadow which is regarded as an integral part of him. Also his possessions, because of their close association with him, become identified with him.

The making of effigies, often of wax, for hostile purposes was common in many ancient and modern cultures, including those of Persia, India, Egypt, Africa and Europe. The Egyptian figures were frequently of the monster Apep, the terrifying opponent of the sun. The papyrus of Nesi-Amsu, now in the British Museum, contains a series of spells to overthrow Apep. To ensure this his name was written in green ink on his effigy which was then wrapped in a piece of new papyrus and thrown on the fire. As it burned it was kicked four times with the left foot. (Similarly the offerings to the Vedic goddess Nirṛti were always pushed towards her with the left foot, indicating her association with the sinister or darker side of life.) The ashes of the burnt figure of Apep were mixed with excrement (representing a worthless offering) and thrown into another fire. Alternatively the effigy was pierced with an arrow through the heart, which by means of 'sympathetic magic' was believed to kill Apep; or a wax figure was held over a fire until it melted. An inverse process was used by Babylonian medico-magicians to rid their patients of malignant devils. A replica was made of the patient, and charms recited to induce the demon to leave him and enter the effigy. Hebrew priests also removed the demon of sickness from patients either into a wax figure or into a slaughtered kid.[25] According to an Ethiopian legend the Virgin Mary was believed to work cures by means of wax figures. Models of wounded men were put in her shrine and offerings made to her. She then caused the wounds to disappear from the figures, and consequently from the wounded men. The Assyrians used effigies to prevent attacks by ghosts; the name of the dead person (i.e., the ghost) was written on a clay image and placed in a gazelle's horn and buried near a caper-bush. In Scotland a similar clay effigy called a *Corp Creadh* was used. Pins were stuck in it wherever the victim was to suffer pain. In Ireland the figures were sometimes made of wheat fashioned to resemble a human body, with a heart of plaited straw; pins were stuck in the joints. The image-maker then went to church, recited certain prayers with his back to the altar, after which he buried the effigy in the devil's name near his victim's house. According to the *Maqlû* series (ii.113) small magical figures were made of *lî* (dung) to counteract sorcery.[26]

Wooden figures of enemies were also made and particular rites carried out to ensure their destruction. One such rite prescribes that a man desirous of removing an enemy should fast for three days, commencing on the fourteenth day of the dark half of the month. He should then stand in a burial ground (*śmaśāna*) on a spot sloping southwards [towards the region of the dead], wearing a red headband, carrying a sword and using *bilva* wood for fuel. For seven days mustard-oil and salt are poured into the fire. Then with logs from the 'royal tree' (*rājavṛkṣa*) the verses of *RV.* III.53,21–4, expressing hatred of the Vasiṣṭhas, are uttered. At night he makes an image of his enemy in *śamyāka* wood (Cathartocarpus fistula Pers.); performs a sacrifice, using the image, and again muttering the above Ṛgvedic verses says: 'this [person] is the oblation' – and within a week his enemy will die (*Ṛgvidhāna* II.4.5; 4.1ff.). These verses were formerly uttered by Kuśika. (The great sage Viśvāmitra, the opponent and rival of Vasiṣṭha, was a descendant of Kuśika.) But the *Bṛhaddevatā* IV.118f. states that the verses were pronounced by Viśvamītra and are traditionally held to be imprecations (*abhiśāpa*) and magical incantations (*abhicārika*) against enemies. So powerful were they that no one was safe from a person who muttered them. The Vasiṣṭhas, realizing their power, refused to listen to them, because great guilt and danger culminating in death arises from repeating or hearing them. Even the children of those who hear them will die.

In an atharvanic rite against *rākṣasas* (demons) the ritual directs the suppliant to eat a rice [milk] pudding or porridge boiled over birds' nests, the smell of which placates demons. Indra is invoked and *soma* pressed for him which so exhilarates him that he drives away the *rākṣasas*. In another charm (*AV.* VIII.4) he is implored to make the sorcerer 'non-existent'. This is similar in intention to the Voodoo-Christian prayer recited when the most fearful of the black arts – the 'sending of the dead' against an enemy – is practised. The image of St Expedit is placed upside down and the Saint invoked:

> Almighty God, my Father, come and find so-and-so that he may be 'disappeared (*sic*) before me like the thunder and lightning. Saint Expedit . . . I call on you and take you as my patron from today, I am sending you to find so-and-so; rid me of . . . his head, rid me of his memory . . . of all my enemies, visible and invisible, bring down on them thunder and lightning. In thine honour Saint Expedit, three Paters.[27]

This folk-motif of 'sending' also appears in Icelandic folk-tales, where an animal, a corpse, or a magically endowed bone which could change shape, would be 'sent against' enemies by the sorcerer. In *AV.* VIII.4 dog-sorcerers (*śvayātu*) are mentioned, and may allude to dogs being the familiars of witches, as they were in European witchcraft.[28]

When a person knows that a curse has been laid on him he invokes the personified 'thousand-eyed' Curse to destroy his curser as quickly as lightning destroys a tree (*AV.* VI.37). This notion derives from the concept that every word of 'a curse consolidates into real matter and can never be annihilated, before it has become true, though later on it may be counter-balanced by an equally effective second thought or word. . . From this magical concept of thought results the later ethical precept . . . that wickedness in thought and speech must be as equally avoided as sin in deeds.'[29] A curse is much more than a mere wish to do harm; it is an actual means of conveying injury by word or act. Thus we speak of 'blistering' invective. The Hebrews, Canaanites and other Semites believed that a curse was the magical release of supernatural power against those hated by God and man; both blessings and curses were indestructible, and hence Isaac, who had blessed Jacob in mistake for Esau, was unable to nullify the words or prevent their fulfilment. Blessings and curses are in essence the same, depending on the intention of the agent. In a curious passage in the New Testament (Gal. 3:13) Christ is said to have 'become a curse for us'; and in an Old Testament passage (Num. 5:18ff.) reference is made to 'curse-bringing water'. In Nigeria witch-doctors keep a cursing apparatus always with them, consisting of some unspecified materials rolled tightly into a ball of black cloth and tied with white thread. Whenever occasion demands it, a powerful curse can be 'blown' in the direction of an enemy.

The curse-effacing ritual attached to *AV.* VI.37 prescribes that a 'pale' (white) lump (*piṇḍam pāṇḍum*) of some now unknown substance should be given to a dog. An oblation of *iṅgiḍa*-oil (always used in hostile rites) is poured out and faggots laid on the fire. The Assyrians 'drove away' curses by burning garlic, dates, hair and wool. The present-day

Yorubas of Africa believe that personal ill-will can be conveyed through carefully prepared and delivered curses, 'or through the manipulation of various magical devices which enable hatred and envy to act effectively across time and space'.[30]

Although some so-called witch-doctors use poisons to ensure that their prophecies, divinations and curses come true, many of their followers have such complete faith in their powers that any material aids are unnecessary. This faith is largely created by the complex ceremonies undergone by initiates in an atmosphere calculated to inspire fear and an uncritical belief in the death-dealing power of curses. The man who has been cursed enters a state of acute anxiety which disturbs his body and metabolic functions and he dies of 'fright'.[31] This is similar to the 'magical fright' (*susto*) experienced by many tribes throughout Latin America, which is an intense psychic trauma induced by fear.

In Vedic charms and spells a number of divinities and ritual entities are called upon to protect the suppliant from harm. They include the Āditya (the all-seeing sun), and the all-healing plant formerly used by the ancient *ṛṣi* Kaṇva, to overcome pests and demons (*AV.* VI.52); the power of the oblation (*nairbādhyam havis*) to suppress enemies (VI.75); the rising sun to take away the lustre (*tejas*) of the stars and also the strength of those sleeping after sunrise (regarded as sinful), and to transfer to the supplicant the 'splendour', that is, the merits, wealth and other qualities of those who hate him (VII.13). The ritual uses the last charm to render enemies powerless, the second verse being uttered whilst gazing steadfastly at them. Gonda points out that 'the effect of a destructive action in the ritual sphere is enhanced when it is accompanied by a look directed towards the object [or person] . . . a look was consciously regarded as a form of contact.'[32]

To invalidate a sacrifice performed by an enemy the ritual (*Kauś.* 48,27) uses *AV.* VII.70 and VI.54, and implores the goddess of destruction Nirṛti to ally herself with Death, and to destroy the enemy's offering before his sacrificial rite can take effect. Merely by performing a sacrifice an enemy gains the power and strength of a non-sacrificer (*Tait. Saṁ.* II.2.9,3). To avert such a calamity the latter should offer a special kind of sacrifice in which the offering is made *before* any words are uttered, thus he forestalls and 'gains' for himself all the speech of his adversary. The so-called *vihavya* prayer (V.3) is closely related to the above two *AV.* charms. The name *vihavya* is derived from the word *vihava* 'call', meaning to call in different directions, i.e., a 'conflicting call'. This was an early witchcraft practice designed to attract the gods to one's own sacrifice and consequently away from the sacrificial rites of others.

Although many of these magical practices may seem absurd in a technological age, they are of the utmost importance in unsophisticated societies where they provide an unfailing guide to action in times of crisis, thereby releasing the tensions and stresses of the individual or the community – stresses caused by fear, disease, conflicts, natural disasters and other misfortunes – so giving man hope and the courage to carry on. In such societies the idea of coincidence is little developed, every occurrence being thought to have a definite cause. Furthermore, the magical view of nature gave rise to the belief that there was a general connexion between human and celestial affairs, a view which lasted until the scientific revolution of the seventeenth century.

EIGHT

Expiatory rites and charms

Many expiatory rites stem from the Indo-Iranian period. They were intended to propitiate the gods and demons and to make reparation and thereby remove the effects of wrong-doing incurred by infringement of the brahmanic social or religious codes; to avert or neutralize inauspicious omens; and to nullify the effects of unusual occurrences, such as the birth of human or animal twins. It was also necessary to avert the terrifying effects of bad dreams and nightmares. In fact anything that was frightening or harmful to man was regarded as the work of powerful supernatural forces which it was necessary to placate and then to make reparation by expiating the wrongful deeds committed.

The people believed implicitly in the efficacy of symbolic actions which required a highly developed ritual. To them wrong-doing usually involved carrying out forbidden acts. (The notion of individual morality did not come until later.) They felt themselves surrounded by demonic forces which inflicted all manner of calamities, including the raping of women and the subsequent birth of monsters and other abnormal offspring; hence sexual relationships were subject to innumerable prohibitions. But even after taking great care a 'tabu' might be involuntarily broken which would render a person vulnerable to demonic attacks. In such an event a priest was called upon to exorcize the demon and to transfer it to another person, animal, bird or object. Such exorcisms were the basis of the 'atonement' (i.e. reparation) principle which stemmed from a primitive notion that a surrogate must be provided for the demon, such as the Gadarene swine into which Jesus drove the devils exorcized from the possessed man. In the Old Testament the Hebrews drove out the scapegoat, loaded with their sins, to placate the demon Azazel. The Bible states that 'no expiation can be made for the land for the blood that is shed therein, but by way of him that shed it' (Num. 35:33; and see Lev. 17:11). Most Christians believe 'that the blood of Christ alone can expiate sin'.[1]

Tertullian, Origen and other early Church Fathers believed that Jesus' disciples could also control demons by muttering His name – a power passed down to the ordained clergy. Today every Roman Catholic priest 'receives previous consecration to the lower orders, including that of exorcist'.[2] Also in some Churches of the United Kingdom and in many of the African Churches, clerics take part in exorcist rites, often with dreadful results as in the recent Michael Taylor case.

Confession of wrong-doing is advocated in some texts, including the *Ṛgvidhāna* (III.4,5), which states that a man who slays a brahman must *inter alia* 'communicate' (confess) 'his deed [and] wander about for twelve years, bearing a skull and a club shaped like the foot of a bedstead and covered in a cloth of bark'. The *ŚBr.* (II.5.2,20; see also *Manu* XI,228) states that a sin (*enas*) once confessed becomes less, since by confession it is transformed into truth (*satya*). Some confessional verses of a general character are included in the *RV.* (VII.86,5; 89,5).

Many expiatory rites were extremely painful and even fatal; that for drinking *surā* (a spiritous liquor) necessitated the guilty man drinking hot liquid until his inside was scalded; only then was his guilt expiated (*Manu* XI.91ff.). Alternative expiations include the following: he could offer himself as a target for archers, thus shortening the expiatory period; or he could throw himself thrice into a blazing fire;

or institute a horse-sacrifice (*aśvamedha*) (*Manu* XI.100ff.).

The boundary between religious and secular law was not clearly defined, and kings inflicted secular punishments and also dictated penances for the expiation of religious offences. Even as late as 1875 the ruler of Kashmir personally ensured that the expiations prescribed by the five learned jurists of the country were duly carried out.[3]

The five products of the cow – milk, curds, ghee, urine and dung – figure prominently in expiatory rites because of the sacred character and veneration which the Indo-Aryans accorded to the cow, because it supplied most of the essentials of life for them, as sheep did for the ancient Hebrews. Cows were regarded as the most auspicious purifiers and on them the sacrifice depends, since they provide the milk and ghee which constitute the basis of the sacrificial offerings; the very continuance of the world-process was believed to depend on the correct and regular performance of sacrifices. Furthermore, the terrestrial cows were regarded as the counterparts of Indra's own celestial cattle (*RV.* V.3,3), an association which further intensified their special sanctity. The *Agni Purāṇa* (II. p. 1075), a post-Vedic work, states that even a drop of water falling from the horn of a cow will expiate all sins, and the *Viṣṇu Sūtra* (xxiii,56ff.) that penitents desiring expiation should rub themselves with water which has fallen from the horns of a cow. Cow urine is specially purifying, being a concentrate of all the nutritive powers of the auspicious animal. Everything associated with the cow is beneficial to man, including even the dust from its hoofprints, which was efficacious in driving away evil spirits from the infant Kṛṣṇa, and hence dried cow-dung is sometimes placed on the heads of children to prevent them from being possessed by malignant spirits. The Ionian philosopher Heraclitus, when suffering from dropsy, is reputed to have buried himself in a cow-stall so that 'the dropsy would be evaporated . . . by the heat of the manure'.[4] A belief in the curative properties of cow-dung poultices was common in rural England up to the end of the nineteenth century.

Sin can be a conscious act performed in opposition to the laws of the gods and of the universe; it can also be transferable from man to man, father to son,[5] and from gods to man, for the sins of the gods affect man. The *AV.* contains over forty expiatory charms to neutralize the bad effects of physical defects – insanity, disease, nightmares, mishaps, accidents, the performance of sorcery, ill-omens, the Evil Eye, errors in the performance of sacrificial rites, offences against social and religious rules, crimes consciously or unconsciously committed, and non-payment of debts. According to the *Ṛgvidhāna* (III.25,2), *RV.* (X.88) is the most efficacious expiatory text, and when uttered averts evil, and expiates and purifies the reciter from sin.

Since prehistoric times particular birds have been regarded as the harbingers of good or bad luck. Black or nocturnal birds were naturally associated with disaster and death; in nineteenth-century Wales many farmers killed any black animals or chickens which came into their possession; their colour, being that of Satan, indicated that evil spirits dwelt in them. Whilst such animals were being killed their owners knelt and prayed. Three atharvanic charms (VI.27 to 29) are directed against inauspicious birds, especially the dove, called the 'winged missile', the messenger of the goddess of destruction, Nirṛti. She, like the Greek Nemesis, also punishes the violators of the laws of Nature. The ill-omened bird speeds towards its victim like an arrow; thus it must be propitiated, expiated and driven away by sacred formulas (mantras).

The *Bṛhaddevatā* (VIII.67ff.) relates that the seer Kapota (whose name means dove) and Nairṛta (son of Nirṛti) practised prolonged asceticism (*tapas*) in the forest. One day a dove placed its claw on his fire-pan; immediately the seer praised the bird, so expiating and averting the bad luck which would otherwise have followed. Even the sight of the bird's claw-marks in the ashes of the hearth is an ill-omen, since the dove – called Yamadūta – is the messenger of Death. In the West doves were thought by some to be the reincarnated dead and hence they often figured as death-omens. In France a sick person who wished to eat pigeon flesh was said to be near death. In England the presence of pigeons formerly indicated death, especially if they settled on the roof. Welsh miners also regarded them as death omens when they flew over the pit-head.

In another charm (*AV*. VI.28) to counteract the effects of the ill-omened dove, the auspicious and luck-bringing cow is led round the household fire, probably to obliterate the ominous claw-marks of the dove on the ashes of the hearth; fire is then carried round the house for purificatory purposes. Another inauspicious bird, the owl (*ulūka*), is also referred to, its screeching being an evil omen. This bird is especially uncanny because of its strange silent flight, so different from the noisy fluttering of other birds.

According to the *RV*. (VII.104,22) fiends may assume many shapes, including that of a dog, cuckoo, owl or owlet. To the Assyrians and other Semites, the owl was also a bird of ill-omen and associated with demons. In the Bible (Lev.11:15f.) the dove and owl are both unclean; to the Romans and Syrians it was a funerary bird. The Roman term *striges* for the horned owl was also applied to witches; the Malagasy call it the 'spirit bird' which embodies the spirits of the dead; the Ainus of Japan fear that its hooting can bewitch. But the Siberian Enets shamans are assisted by owls in their struggles with evil spirits.

Europeans consider the owl unlucky, especially if it flies round a house or perches on the roof; in parts of rural Ireland owls are killed as soon as they enter a house, because if allowed to fly away they would carry with them the 'luck of the household'. The owl is the death-bird (*merimásko cerikclo*) of the gypsies, and the 'corpse-bird' of the Welsh. The Yorubas of Nigeria regard it as a witch-bird – sent by sorcerers to kill their enemies. If the bird gets into a house the inmates catch it and break its wings and claws, thinking thereby to injure the sorcerer who sent it. But some Bantus fear even to touch it because of its close association with hostile witchcraft. Many American Indian tribes associated it with the dead; in Ojibwa belief the dead pass over the 'owl bridge' to reach the next world.

Nightmares and evil dreams were greatly feared by the Indians and others, and hence required expiation. The Mesopotamians had a god of dreams called Zaqar, the 'terror of the nights', who is paralleled by the 'terror by night' of the Biblical Song of Songs.[6] The Assyrian nightmare was *alû*, and is the same as the Arabic *ḳabus* that throws itself heavily on a sleeper and so prevents him moving. This was a form of the incubus which so occupied the minds of medieval European demonologists and churchmen. There was also a malady called Incubus by the Latins.[7]

Evil dreams were sometimes successively consigned to Trita (a divinity who dwelt in the remotest part of the heavens), to Dvita and to the Dawn whose welcome light drives away bad dreams (*RV.* VIII.47,15ff.); another *sūkta* (X.164) called *duhsvapnanāśana* wards off evil dreams; and X.127 dedicated to Rātrī (night) expiates bad dreams or an evil omen such as the unusual and hence ominous sound of a crow heard in the dead of night. The expiation for a terrifying nightmare requires an offering of a cake of mixed grain, and a second cake placed on land belonging to an enemy; the bad dream is transferred to the second cake which will then bring trouble to one's enemy. But the best protection from nightmares was sound sleep – called the immortal child of the gods (*AV.* VI.47) – whose mother was the goddess Varuṇānī, and whose father, Yama, ruled the dead.

AV. VI.112 is designed to expiate the much dreaded bad effects of inversion of precedence, when a younger brother marries before an elder brother. This affects both brothers adversely, and the god Pūṣan is invoked to let the bad effects pass to an abortionist (or perhaps to the demon who destroys embryos). The inversion of precedence also applied to Hebrew women, a younger sister being forbidden to marry before an elder sister, thus Leah was substituted for Rachel (Gen. 29:15ff.).

AV. VI.112 and 113 are associated with Trita, the 'scapegoat' of the gods. According to the *Maitri Saṁhitā*, IV.1,9, the gods were unable to find a suitable being on whom to 'wipe off' their own guilt derived from 'the bloody part of the sacrifice' until Agni spat on the waters from which then arose the three Āptya deities – Ekata, Dvita and Trita, to whom the gods transferred their guilt, and who in turn passed it on to various wrongdoers. The *ŚBr.* (I.3,3) version relates that the Āptya deities, who often accompanied Indra, were with him when he slew the brahmin Viśvarūpa, Tvaṣṭṛ's son, and hence they became 'accessories to the crime' of brahminicide. Subsequently, the Āptyas transferred the guilt to those persons who fail to give *dakṣiṇās* ('gifts') to the priests. The *Kauś. Sūtra* mentions twelve sins which were transferred to man. (Twelve is a round number often used in ancient ritual.) The human body was also believed to consist of twelve parts, a notion also well attested among the Hittites. The *Kauś.* states that finally the sin of inversion of precedence was transferred to the *muñja* grass (*Saccharum muñja*), which is then tied to the limbs of the two brothers suffering from the effects (i.e., illness) of the sin. Whilst they are seated on a river-bank the priest washes them down with more bunches of grass dipped in water and then places grass fetters (symbolizing the illness) in the river which carries them and the illness away.

The ancient world was much preoccupied with the effects of blood guilt, the blood of a murdered man was said to shriek from the ground – a belief still current among some Arabs. The Old Testament relates that Abel's blood cried to God from the earth. Bloodshed was supposed to pollute the earth and necessitated expiation. Even hunters were required to cover up the spilt blood of beasts or fowls (Lev. 17:13). The Aryan settlers in Vedic India were much given to blood sacrifices, but most Hindus have never felt at ease about them, as *AV.* II.34 implies. It is a prayer recited during the sacrifice of an animal, and is an attempt to rationalize it. The priests asserted that the animal was actually unharmed by its execution, and furthermore that it willingly assented to its own death![8] In some mysterious way, it is ransomed from death that it may follow its own sinless sacrificer to the celestial world. Similarly in the *ŚBr.* (III.7.4,5ff.), the sacrificial animal's kin and others of the herd are said to give their approval to the slaying!

An important expiation is that made for errors which occurred in sacrificial ritual (*AV.* VI.114), which could have grave consequences. The priests pray for forgiveness for having committed any deeds which may have angered the gods; the Ādityas are invóked to release the priests from the anger of the gods, since the priests desired only to accomplish a perfect sacrifice, but had failed.

An expiatory formula for sins consciously or unconsciously committed calls upon the gods to release the sinner as if from a [sacrificial?] post (*AV.* VI.115). For a man to expiate unknown evils incurred unwittingly, he must rise early and continually cleanse himself whilst uttering specific mantras (*Ṛgvidhāna* III.6,4–5). The personified household fire (Agni gārhapatya) is also invoked to lead the sinner *away* from sin to the heavenly world (*AV.* VI.120). In the *Tait. Saṁ.* (I.8.5,3), the *gārhapatya* fire and the personified Sky are invoked so that the worshipper may attain the celestial world where no illness or deformities exist, and where parents and children are reunited.

Agni gārhapatya is also invoked to expiate the defilement (regarded as a sinful state) caused by something dropped by an ill-omened black-plumaged bird, with which the goddess of destruction, Nirṛti, is equated (*AV.* VII.64). Nirṛti's form is black (*Tait. Saṁ.* V.2,4), and hence black garments, ornaments and objects are used in her rites since she represents the dark side of life. In post-Vedic works she became associated with witchcraft and was invoked by those wishing to attain magical powers (*Bhāgavata Purāṇa* 2,3,1ff.).

Three 'hymns' emphasize the word *ṛṇa* (debt), referring to unpaid debts (*AV*. VI.117 to 119). The first appears to refer to debts due to one's fellow men and to the gods. Agni is invoked to make the supplicant guiltless (*anṛṇa* – 'free from debt or obligation'), and by extension from blame or fault. This is clearly brought out by a variant reading in the *Tait. Saṁ*. III.3.8, If.: 'That loan which I have not yet paid back, the tribute that I still owe to Yama, here do I make requital for it; here O Agni, may I be freed from that debt.' The second apparently deals with unpaid gambling debts and invokes the two fierce *apsarasas* (nymphs) to forgive the guilt of the gambler, these nymphs being closely associated with games of chance, especially dicing.

Among the various expiations is one to make reparation for the offences caused by the activities of ploughmen who 'wound the earth'. Failure to do so leads to death. Other expiations were prescribed to make reparation for the accidental spilling of sacrificial liquids; the *Aitareya Brāhmaṇa*, 7.9,3, uses *RV*. IX.83, the purifying mantra (*śodhanamantra*), to expiate errors in sacrificial ritual; the uttering of the *Sāmavidhāna Brāhmaṇa* (1.5,15) expiates the sin of drinking intoxicants.

The *apāmārga* plant (*Achyranthes aspera*) found all over India is often used for expiatory and purificatory purposes. Its leaves are long and retroflected and hence it is called the 'reverted one' (*punaḥsara*). It is magically efficacious both in 'wiping off' curses and causing them to 'revert' to the curser; it is addressed as follows: 'O apāmārga, drive away from us sin, guilt, witchery, infirmity and evil dreams!' (*ŚBr*. XIII.8.4,4). By means of this plant the gods removed the fiends (*rākṣasas*) from the four quarters of the world (V.2.4,14). When the sacrificer and officiants return to the sacrificial area the suppliant prays that his enemies, wherever they may be, shall be driven away; he then makes an offering whilst looking back, 'for the *apāmārga* is of backward effect' (V.2.4,20).

Among other expiatory charms are those for sins committed through forgetfulness and consequent neglect of religious duties (*AV.* VII.106); to regain sacred knowledge lost through sinning, such as studying the sacred texts in the wrong place or at the wrong time, or in cloudy weather, or in sight of green barley, or within the hearing of cattle (VII.66 and 67).

A man who urinates when standing erect commits a sin which requires expiation, as it offends the gods of Heaven and Earth, and those of the Atmosphere and of Death (*AV.* VII.102), and hence the Indian peasants adopt the squatting position when urinating. Anyone urinating facing the sun, or who kicks a cow, will be 'hewn off at the root' (*AV.* XIII.1,56). The *Viṣṇu Sūtra* LX.1ff. includes a number of rules regarding urination and defecation, among which are the following: not facing the wind, fire, moon, sun, or before a woman, guru or a brahmin.

Expiation is necessary for such unlucky occurrences as a child being born at an inauspicious time or under an unlucky star (*AV.* VI.110); or the unusual event of a child's first two upper teeth appearing before the lower. The teeth themselves are believed to be inherently dangerous and hence must be placated. They are urged to be content with rice, barley, beans, sesame and similar foods, and not to injure the child's parents. The charm ends with the words: 'O ye teeth, let what is injurious in yourselves depart; do not injure father and mother.' The ritual (*Kauś.* 46,43–6) prescribes that the child be made to bite the above foods, and then both child and parents eat grain previously boiled in consecrated water. A number of other unusual occurrences must also be expiated, such as the presence of a barren cow in a herd (*AV.* XII.4); a drop of water falling unexpectedly from a clear sky; or fruit falling on a person from a tree. The part of the body or clothing on which the water or fruit fell must be purified so as to 'thrust perdition (Nirṛti) away' (*AV.* VI.124). In Judaism rain falling out of season was considered harmful (Ez. 13:13).

NINE

Charms for prosperity

In a predominantly rural economy the possession of cattle and land was essential for prosperity, and resulted in cattle being the standard of value until the introduction of coinage.[1] The only means of augmenting the natural increase of the community's herds, was by cattle-raiding (*gaviṣṭi*), or by their capture in affrays with neighbouring tribes, and hence Indra, the Aryan war-god, was invoked to give his worshippers cattle and thus make them prosperous (*RV.* V.42,2). Cattle were also the chief source of food in early Vedic times as well as providing various useful by-products as they do today, including dung, some of which is used as fertilizer, some as cooking fuel, and when made into a paste and smeared over a dirt floor and allowed to harden provides a smooth surface easily kept clean. Marvin Harris[2] states that the excreta of India's cattle provides about 700 million tons of manure, and the annual quantity of heat obtained from it 'is the thermal equivalent of 27 million tons of kerosene, 35 million tons of coal, or 68 million tons of wood', so indicating that even barren cows have their uses, particularly as Indian cattle live largely by scavenging.

As any form of wealth attracts the attention of the thief, the envious and the greedy, specific spells were employed by the atharvan priests on behalf of the 'wealthy', or in some cases by the suppliants themselves.

Against loss incurred by natural calamities, unseasonable

weather conditions and so forth, the agriculturist relied on the favour of the gods and spirits. But for anything involving pure chance, Lakṣmī (also called Srī), the goddess of fortune and good luck, was invoked.

The *sāṁsrāvya havis* – the oblation said to cause cattle, rivers and birds to 'flow together', thereby increasing wealth – naturally played an important role in achieving general prosperity (*AV.* I.15; II.26; XIX.1). This 'flowing together' also increased the power of the sacrifice and its benefits. An increase of power was believed to emanate from any animals, persons or objects when doubled or paired – a notion stemming from the observation that from the union of a human or an animal couple, other beings may be born. Thus a pair signifies both strength as well as procreative ability.

Vedic dwellings were constructed of bamboo and were easy both to erect and pull down. An elaborate ritual for the erection of a building is given in the *Kauś. Sūtra* (43,3ff.; *AV.* VII.41), part of which is devoted to facilitating the task of the builder. After placing the king-post and cross-beam in position, the house was 'clothed', i.e. roofed – either with sods of grass or thatched. A water-vessel was taken inside and a fire lit, the latter symbolizing the luck of the house, like the horseshoe hung up on farmhouse doors and stables in the West. In India the figure of Lakṣmī is often depicted on the doors and lintels of houses to ensure good luck and to avert adverse influences. As soon as the house was erected it was deified and regarded as a living entity since the welfare of its inhabitants now depended on it. When entering the new house the housewife carried a vessel of ghee (*ghṛta*) and ambrosia (*amṛta*), symbolizing abundance, fertility and longevity.

Like most closely knit communities Vedic families were very loath to leave their homes and household divinities. They may be compared to Rachel who, despite the pleas of Jacob, refused to leave her Aramaean home without her household gods (Gen. 31:19ff.). The affection for the house is expressed in *AV.* VII.60, where the owner's manner when approaching it is likened to a meeting of old friends. Before setting out on a long journey, the owner spoke reassuringly to it and promised to return with gifts that would increase the well-being of its occupants.

Veneration for a house is reflected in the Palestinian 'sacrifice between the feet' performed on behalf of its owner when returning from Mecca, or for someone who has been long absent. The returning traveller stood before the door with legs apart. A sheep or goat was placed between his feet, its throat cut and some blood put on his forehead. If the pilgrim was a Christian the mark of the cross was made on his forehead in blood.[3]

Each house has its tutelary goddess (representing the Earth) who is called upon to protect the household and endow it with wealth and heroic sons. The house has also a tutelary deity, Vāstoṣpati, who with the goddess is expected to drive away any evil spirits that may gain entry.[4] Vāstoṣpati is called upon to prevent disease entering the homestead and to make the inhabitants and their kine prosper (*RV.* VII.54 and 55). The epithet 'lord of the house' (Vāstoṣpati) is also applied to Indra who initially may have been a house-guardian. The hearth is the domain of Agni who lies within the house like an embryo. To prevent the house burning down aquatic lotus flowers and water are kept in it – a common device in magical texts for protection against fire.

When lands were cultivated communally it was customary to have an annual division of crops and cattle among the community's adult males. The god Bhaga 'the Dispenser' (of wealth, and counterpart of the Iranian Baga) was invoked to ensure an impartial division. Even the tribal chieftain or village headman was beholden to Bhaga for his share, and hence the god's honorifics, Bhagavant 'Sharer' and Vidhātar 'Disposer'. As the division inevitably resulted in anomalies – one man getting better cattle than another, or a more fertile strip of land – each member of the community worshipped Bhaga in the hope of getting a good share for himself. This, however, is at variance with the myth that Bhaga was blind and thus completely impersonal in the sharing out of tribal goods.

A number of charms are concerned with the protection, increase and welfare of cattle, further indicating their importance to the Vedic economy. None the less, despite the desire for fertile cows, the birth of twin calves was feared as being an unnatural event and hence an unfavourable portent both for the cow and for the herd (*AV.* III.28) which required expiation. In addition to protecting cattle from disease, they needed to be protected against thieves, wild animals, and the 'toothed rope', as snakes were called (*AV.* IV.3). To ensure their protection, the ritual (*Kauś.* 51,1ff.) prescribes that the herdsman should follow the trail of the cattle whilst alternately raising and driving a stake of *khadira* wood into the ground. Such actions were thought actually to pierce the tracks of any hostile animals or beings likely to attack the herds. *Khadira* wood is frequently used in magical rites, largely because of its etymology which means 'devour'. Thus in *AV.* VIII.8,3, it says: 'devour (*khād*) [yonder men] speedily, O *khadira*'. Oblations of ghee poured into a fire of this wood gives a thousand-fold gain (*Ṛgvidhāna* II.7,1).

Protective charms and amulets for livestock are common in many cultures, including the Sumerian, Babylonian, Egyptian, Mediterranean and European. The belief in the 'hexing' of cattle existed among the Pennsylvania Germans up to the first quarter of this century. The horse brasses of the United Kingdom were originally intended as protective devices; whilst today the human animal is protected by St Christopher medals, crucifixes, the *ankh* (the ancient Egyptian symbol of life), rabbits' feet, tigers' claws, lucky mascots and so forth.

To ensure the well-being of cattle the priest prays that they may be healthy and have comfortable stalls (*AV.* III.14) close to their owner. In many parts of rural Europe almost to the present day man shared his home with his domestic animals, and in parts of Ireland, Scotland and Wales, it is still held that 'warmth increases the yield of milk' and that the 'cow must see the fire'.[5] The cattle are commanded to flock together without fear, making rich manure and multiplying like *śaka* (dung). The emphasis on dung may have some connexion with the great Neolithic ash-mounds of burnt cow-dung studied by F. R. Allchin, who points out that the Kanada word *būdi* (ash) occurs in place-names to signify ash-mounds, and also occurs in the name of the full-moon day (*būdi pūrnimā*) of the Holī festival. On such an occasion the dung fires were probably lighted, resulting in the production of masses of dung-ash (*vibhūti*),[6] so turning the cow-pens into auspicious areas. Even in pre-Vedic times the fires may have been part of even more widespread 'cattle-rites, and thus through the millennia the sacred ashes of cow-dung have survived as a surrogate of the ash-mound cult'.[7] According to the *Ṛgvidhāna* (III.13,2), a man wishing to gain more cattle should repeat mantras in a cow-pen, or pour oblations into a fire after fasting.

Many modern Indian seasonal and pastoral festivals are linked in a general manner with ancient customs. Cattle were driven through or between fires during the Holī and Dīvālī festivals, as they were during the Celtic May Day Festival of Beltane, a survival of an early pastoral festival accompanying the turning-out of the herds to pasture. The fires protected them against disease and the attacks of demonic beings.

To establish ownership of cattle it was customary to cut or 'punch' their ears (*AV.* VI.141), a practice that has lasted to the present day. Two sets of marks appear to have been made on each animal, one resembling the shape of the genitals, a magical device to ensure their fertility, the other being the owner's mark. A red knife (probably of copper, a metal associated with fertility in Tantrism) was used to make the special genitalia mark on both ears – a mark said to have been instituted by the *asuras*, the gods and the twin Aśvins.

But whoever dares to punch (*ā-sku*) the ears of a priest's cow with his own mark, intending to claim it for himself, incurs the wrath of the gods (*AV*. XII.4,6).[8]

Keeping the land in good heart involved adequately manuring and ploughing it before sowing, and when followed by rain and sunshine, a good harvest was ensured. Hence the sun was called the 'Fattener' (*Tait. Saṁ*. III.3.8,6). Ploughing was the most arduous task of the Vedic agriculturist, the ploughs being heavy and cumbersome and requiring – according to the nature of the soil – from six to twelve oxen and sometimes more, but the farmers, realizing that man is part of nature (a fact overlooked in the Semitic religions), were anxious not to over-exploit the soil, and hence had specific rites to expiate the harm done and so make amends for disturbing the earth.

The plough and ploughshare were personified as the dual agricultural deities Śunāsīra[9] and the goddess Sītā (Indra's wife) personified as the Furrow, regarded as the Earth's womb.[10] Indra, in common with all solar gods, became a vegetal deity and hence was worshipped by agriculturists (*Taittirīye Br*. II.4.7,2; II.4.3,11). In other texts he is called Śunāsīra (*Tait. Saṁ*. I.8,7; *Bṛhadd*. 5,8) and Urvarāpati, 'lord of the field' (*RV*. VIII.21,3). The *sūkta* (*RV*. IV.57) 'seen' by the *ṛṣi* Vāmadeva is addressed to the lord of the field, Kṣetrapati, who is invoked to bestow cattle on his worshippers. According to the *Bṛhadd*. 5,9f. verse 8 of the above *sūkta* 'praises' agriculture and so stimulates and makes successful the ploughing.[11] The *sūkta* ends with the words 'Grant us prosperity, Śuna and Sīra'.

There is evidence that ploughing was known to the Indians before they separated from the Iranians, since similar agricultural terms are included in the *Ṛgveda* and *Avesta*. The 'culture-hero' Pṛthi Vainya is credited with being the originator of ploughing (*AV*. VIII.10,24), and the plough itself came to represent wealth (*ŚBr*. VIII.2.2,11).

The twin Aśvins were also associated with agriculture and

invoked to smite insects which 'bore' into grain and fruit, and rats, locusts and other predators and to 'close their mouths' (*AV.* VI.50). To remove mice the ritual (*Kauś.* 51,17ff.) prescribes that the field be scratched with lead (a metal greatly feared by demons), and stones scattered on the field; the mouth of an insect should be tied up with a hair, and the insect buried head downwards in the middle of a field. A *bali* offering (part of a daily offering by householders) is made to Āśā (the personification of a quarter of the heavens) and to Āśāpati, 'lord of the regions', to the Aśvins and to Kṣetrapati, 'lord of the field'; after which the suppliant remains silent until sunset. According to the *Ṛgvidhāna* (II.14,5), rats, mice, and moles must be propitiated with sacrificial offerings of boiled rice placed on a mole-hill. Moles were believed to know the very essence of the earth, and the mounds thrown up by them represent this essence and so bring about good fortune (śrī) (*ŚBr.* II.1.1,7). Agni is also associated with mole-hills, and a myth relates that once when he was hiding from the other gods he burrowed into the earth like a mole; his 'mole-hills' also embody the essence of the earth (*Tait. Br.* I.1.3,3).

Irrigation and the seasonal monsoon rains are vital in India for successful harvests and prosperity. A person wishing to divert a stream into a new irrigation channel should walk along the intended course, pouring out water as he goes and marking the route with tall reeds, whilst saying: 'Here ye waters is your heart . . . Come ye Mighty Ones by the way I am conducting you!' At the point where the stream is to be tapped a piece of gold and a striped frog (resembling an *iṣīkā* reed) are placed, the frog being tied up with blue and red thread. Water is poured over the frog which is then enveloped in an aquatic *avakā* plant over which more water is poured. An expiatory rite is performed, consisting chiefly of oblations to Varuṇa, the god of the waters, to prevent the new channel causing any flooding (*AV.* III.13; *Kauś.* 40,1ff.).

A few rain-spells are included in the *RV.* invoking the gods Mitra and Varuṇa, Soma and Parjanya. One spell required the suppliant to stand facing East, submerged up to the neck in water. He then worships the sun, fasts for five days and recites *RV.* VII.101 and 102, which will ensure a heavy rainfall (*Ṛgvidhāna* II.30,1f.). In other rain-spells (*AV.* IV.15; VI.22; VII.18) the clouds and winds are invoked to unite and produce rain, or the Maruts (storm-gods),[12] Parjanya (the rain-god), Agni, Prajāpati, Varuṇa and nāgas (serpents), are invoked to let the water-courses be filled with green and speckled frogs. Both serpents and Varuṇa are associated with water. To Varuṇa belong all creatures who have drowned. He is also associated with horses like the Avestan rain-god and the Greek sea-god Poseidon. Frogs also are associated with water and the female frog Tādurī is urged to croak and to swim in the midst of the pool to attract rain. Frogs also bring prosperity, perhaps a notion deriving from the fact that their excessive croaking is usually a sign of rain and hence an auspicious portent. When the rains were overdue the ancient *ṛṣi* Vasiṣṭha praised the clouds and then called upon the frogs to assist him (*Nirukta* 9,6 and 7). The Newars of Nepal identify frogs with nāgas and worship them as controllers of rain. Sometimes frogs are placed on hill-tops to attract the rain to the parched earth, but one of the simplest rain-charms of rural India consists of pouring water over a frog. A rain-spell in the *Tait. Saṁ.* (II.4,7) is uttered by the sacrificer whilst he dons a fringed black garment; the priest summons the east wind and symbolically drives away the west wind; *karīra* groats are placed on a black antelope skin and the ends tied together symbolizing the rain-filled black cloud.

Sometimes the god Dhātar is invoked to untie 'the skin-bag of the water of heaven',[13] or the rain-god Parjanya is urged to 'lift up the mighty vessel and pour down water, letting the liberated streams rush forward' (*RV.* V.83,8). Prayers for rain are sometimes said in Christian churches, and were especially frequent in the United Kingdom during the unusually hot summer of 1976.

Sakadruma (personified dung-smoke) is employed in a curious charm (*AV.* VI.128), which is either intended to predict future weather, or is perhaps a method of divining lucky or unlucky days. As a possessive compound the name means 'he of the dung-smoke', that is, one who foretells the future from the smoke of dung, perhaps by inhalation, or by observing the rise and fall of smoke which could give indications of weather conditions. In some parts of the world inhaling smoke of certain burning plants was used to induce trance states, a method of communicating with the spirit world. On the borders of Kashmir the prophets among the Takhas, before uttering their oracular responses, inhale the smoke of smouldering cedar-wood. In Madura female mediums inhale incense smoke to induce trance, even as Apollo's prophetess inhaled the smoke of burning laurel before prophesying.

Some members of the Vedic community engaged in trade, but on a limited scale, unlike that carried on with Sumeria and Egypt by the river-states of Harappa and Mohenjo-daro before their destruction by the Aryans. The *AV.* includes a few charms intended to increase trade. Oblations offered to Agni ensured a hundredfold increase, as well as forgiveness for sins committed when away from home. The oblations also gave protection from those deities who might prevent successful trading.

The charms and spells employed for the recovery of the loss, either of property or of the family fortune, indicate that some members of the community had achieved a high standard of living. Any loss they suffered might have resulted from cupidity, carelessness, laziness, trickery, sudden calamity or possibly gambling. In the latter event an apsaras (a celestial nymph) is invoked to assist the gambler by her magic (*māyā*) (*AV.* IV.38). A 'Gambler's lament' is included in the *RV.* (X.34), in which an unlucky gambler likens the dice to lumps of magic charcoal which, though cold in themselves, yet burn the heart to ashes. Sometimes the dice themselves were commanded to 'bind' the gambler to a 'streak of gain' – the modern 'lucky streak' or 'run of luck'. Gambling became so widespread that the *Arthaśāstra* (III.20) (a treatise on political science traditionally ascribed to Kauṭilya) advocated its official control, to be financed by a tax of 5 per cent on the stakes in addition to a charge for hiring the dice.

A ritual game of dice was played at the consecration of a king (*rājasūya*) during which the king was handed five dice symbolically indicating his invincibility and conquest of the land in the four regions of the compass and the upper region. The prize for the winner (who is always the king) is a dish of rice (*odana* – a symbol of kingship) whereby he indicates his success, wealth and ability to ensure prosperity for his people.

In Iran the war-chariot came into use during the second millennium BC[14] and was a sign of the owner's prosperity and power. Shortly afterwards most of the Indo-Iranian gods were conceived as driving about in chariots, and hence chariots also figure in ritual. To regenerate the productive forces of the cosmos and ensure future prosperity, ritual chariot-races were held on a circular course. The triaga or three-horsed chariot, the chariot itself, the driver and chariot-borne warrior were equated with the six seasons; the parts of the vehicle with the elements of the cosmos, and the whole chariot with the Year (*saṁvatsara*) which represents Totality [and thus a prosperous year] (*AV.* VIII.8,22f.).

To recover lost property of all kinds the god Pūṣan (a form of the Sun-god, the all-seeing watcher over every road and path) is invoked (*AV.* VII.9). The ritual (*Kauś.* 52,12ff.) prescribes that those seeking lost property should wash and anoint their feet and hands and especially scour their right hands before starting the search. Twenty-one pebbles (representing the objects lost) are scattered at a crossroad – considered the best place to shed bad luck and other malevolent influences which will then harmlessly disperse to the four directions. Some form of divination to facilitate the finding of the lost objects may also have been practised with the pebbles.

Many charms concerned with the avoidance of misfortune and other calamities call upon a number of gods as well as on spirits, demons, the *pitṛs* (ancestors), plants, animals, birds, personified rivers, etc. – such a comprehensive invocation was believed to increase the efficacy of the rite. *AV.* XI.6 is of particular interest as it mentions most of the deities current during the compilation of the *Atharvaveda*: Agni, Indra, Aṁśa, Vivasvant, Savitar, Dhātar, Pūṣan, Tvaṣṭar, the twin Aśvins, Brahmaṇaspati, Aryaman, the Ādityas (sun-gods), Parjanya, Soma, Bhava, Śarva, Rudra, Prajāpati, Yama and the Vasus.

Two late charms (*AV.* XIX.7–8) invoke the twenty-eight lunar constellations (*nakṣatras*)[15] for the attainment of wealth; also for protection, when about to set out on a journey, from the effects of ill-omens, such as sneezing, seeing or hearing jackals or other inauspicious animals.

The *mṛgārāṇi* or *mṛgārasūktāni* charms (*AV.* IV.23 to 29), named after their author Mṛgāra, are designed to ward off misfortunes and so leave the way open for a prosperous life. They also invoke many major and minor deities. Number 28 seems to be purely atharvanic, especially as it is addressed to Bhava and Śarva – two of the eight elemental forms of Rudra – who are lords of men and animals. Śarva (the equivalent of the Avestan Saurva) seems to have been a terrifying being both in Iran and in India. The *Tait. Saṁ.* (IV.5) mentions a number of beings called Śarvas who appear to be chthonic divinities.

To ensure a prosperous year the goddess Ekāṣṭakā (personifying the eighth day after the full moon) is invoked. She is the consort of the personified Year, thus by worshipping her the suppliant is able to 'grasp', i.e., gain prosperity during the whole year.[16]

Other divinities and personified powers were sometimes

placated and then appealed to for prosperity, such as Death (personified) in *AV.* VI.13, where homage is paid to Death's weapons. Also worshipped was the mighty goddess Aditi (the personification of the universe), the universal sovereign, the protector and bestower of universal prosperity and well-being (*AV.* VII.6).

TEN

Charms for harmony

The Vedic records provide ample evidence of the ancient Indian seers' awareness of the multiple forces of nature and of the harmonizing principle that governs them. Much of the oldest ritual of all early cultures is an attempt to create a harmonious world and thus validate man's existence. The model of harmony was the movement of the stellar bodies, particularly of the sun and moon, which not only distinguished day and night and measured time, but also, in association with other phenomena, determined the community's welfare. Such phenomena were regarded as suprahuman beings, some beneficent and some maleficent, the aid of the former being sought and the maleficence of the latter averted by appropriate mantras, supplications, formulas, propitiations and prayers to achieve harmony. For this purpose also Varuṇa, the ancient Indo-Iranian god of law and order – who is still reverenced by Zoroastrians[1] – was frequently invoked. But when Mitra, the god of contracts, and Varuṇa are conjoined they mainly represented social and political harmony, not as an ethical ideal but for practical reasons. Similarly the tenth commandment of the Hebrew Decalogue – which forbade the coveting of a neighbour's ox or his wife – was primarily intended to avoid anti-social consequences.

Much misery, harm and discord were created amongst the indigenous peoples with the arrival of the Aryans

(c. 2000 BC) in Iran and in north-west India. The newcomers initially sought to preserve their ethnic identity, especially their light skin colour (*ārya-varṇa*) from being 'polluted' by intermarriage with the dark-skinned (*dasyu-varṇa*) Dravidians, or with the black-skinned proto-Australoids. Indra is said to give 'protection to the Aryan colour' (*RV.* III.34,9). Also linked with ethnic distinction was the language of the Aryans which, as the language of the Veda and sacrificial ritual, was considered sacred; anyone failing to speak it correctly was regarded as inferior. Other causes of discord included disputes over the ownership of land, boundaries, cattle and political unrest.

Harm and discord usually began with the family, and family quarrels were greatly feared, because they were signs that the family was being attacked by Nirṛti, the goddess of discord and destruction; thus serious quarrels necessitated the perfomance of complex expiatory rites.

As early as the *puruṣa sūkta* of the *RV.* (X.90) – which is primarily a creation myth intended to establish the essential unity and independence of all living beings – mankind was divided into four socially separate but dependent categories. Their descending importance is described mythologically – the *brahmaṇa* or priestly class issued from the mouth of the Cosmic Man (Puruṣa); the *rājanya* or *kṣatra*, the regal and warrior class, from his arms; the *vaiśya*, the agriculturist and merchant class, from his thighs; and the *śūdra* or labouring class from his feet, the latter being emblems of activity and strength.

In ancient India, with its numerous vernaculars, individual interests rather than national considerations were paramount; nationalism, in the modern sense, never being envisaged. Terms like 'freedom' and 'equality' also had little, if any, real significance, nor had they until a couple of millennia later. But whatever the differences between ancient and modern Indian social views, one thing unites them: an unswerving belief that harmony among a community – large or small – must begin with the family, especially with husband and wife, and that the creation of harmony entails the exercise of personal discipline, kindness, tact and tolerance.

To overcome family dissensions *AV.* III.30 purports to be the same incantation which formerly had prevented discord among the gods. Such spells, deriving from the ancient past and associated with the gods, were believed to possess great magical potential. The first three verses of the prayer begin:[2]

> Of one heart and of one mind,
> Free from hatred do I make you,
> Take delight in one another,
> As the cow does in her baby calf.
>
> Loyal to his sire the son be,
> Of one mind, too, with his mother;
> Sweet and kindly language ever
> Let the wife speak to her husband.
>
> Brother shall not hate the brother,
> And the sister not the sister,
> Of one mind and of one intent,
> Speak ye words of kindness only.

The prayer continues that the family shall be united and 'yoked together in the same traces', which is equivalent to the English expression 'pulling together'. The ritual (*Kauś.* 12,6–9) directs that a jar of water anointed with the dregs of ghee be carried round disputants. It and a jar of *surā* (an intoxicant) are then poured on to the ground, so indicating the dispersal of the quarrel as the liquids disperse harmlessly into the earth. The disputants also partook of the pickled flesh of a three-year-old cow and of *surā* and water sprinkled with dregs of ghee.

Family discord was sometimes caused by offences against holy men or against the gods; the former is illustrated in the myth of Śaryāta, whose sons pelted the decrepit and ghost-like figure of the *ṛṣi* Cyavana with clods. The *ṛṣi*, enraged by their behaviour, immediately created discord among the Śaryātas, so that father fought son, and brother attacked brother. Only then did Śaryāta realize that such extreme family discord must be a punishment for an offence that he or his family had committed. Finally, having discovered the cause and to make amends or expiation, he offered Cyavana his daughter Śukanyā in marriage (*ŚBr.* IV.1.5,1–8).

In addition to Varuṇa, the gods Soma, Agni, Bṛhaspati, the Vasus, Pūṣan and Vāstoṣpati were invoked to bring about concord. Three other divinities were also called upon for aid – Bhaga (the dispenser and protector of tribal property), Brahmaṇaspati (the lord of prayer and giver of prosperity) (*RV.* I.18,5,etc.) and Triṇāman (Three-named), he being considered by Sāyaṇa to be either the threefold fire – of earth, lightning and sun – or the three terrestrial ritual fires – the *gārhapatya*, *dakṣiṇā* and *āhavanīya* (*AV.* VI.73–4). Bhaga is an epithet also applied to the tribal leader who, according to Aryan custom, annually distributed booty and the products of communal activity among the adult men of the tribe. Thus the divine Bhaga is the embodiment of good fortune, but Dumézil[3] considers that he presides specifically over movable property, especially cattle.

Other charms are designed to achieve success, prominence and superiority in social and political life, and the power to influence others. These themes are treated in more detail in the *AV.* than in the *RV.*, only three references occurring in the latter collection (X.166; 191; 85,43). In the first *sūkta* the supplicant prays that he may be as a bull among his peers and so overcome his enemies, and that he may acquire their strength and skill in war and peace. The second is addressed in part to Saṁjñanam and to Agni who is called upon to gather up all that is precious for his worshipper. Saṁjñanam, who is the personification of harmony in the assembly, is implored to make all those present of 'like mind'. The third is addressed to the solar deity Aryaman (the equivalent of the

Avestan Airyaman, the 'friend' of humanity). The Vedic Aryaman also controls marriage contracts and finds husbands for unmarried girls.

A plant called *pāṭā* is used to overcome an adversary in a public dispute (*AV.* II.27). It was formerly associated with Indra who wore a *pāṭā*-amulet on his arm. He also ate the plant when he conquered the powerful Asuras and Sālāvṛkas. The *pāṭā* (*Clypea hernandifolia*) has a bitter root and is much used in India as a medicament. It was said to have been discovered (or seen) by an eagle and then dug up by a pig, which suggests that it may have been some kind of truffle. Like many other plants to which magical properties are attributed, its name is etymologically suggestive. The ritual (*Kauś.* 38,18–21) directs that while the above charm is being recited the suppliant should approach his adversary from the north-east whilst chewing a root of *pāṭā* which he retains in his mouth when speaking. He ties on his arm an amulet of *pāṭā* root and wears a wreath of seven of its leaves. The north-east region is ritually important as its name *aparājita* means 'unsurpassed', and 'invincible'.

Some charms (*AV.* VI.42 and 43) are employed to remove or assuage Wrath (Manyu) personified, who also figures in battle-charms, because in battle, rage provides the necessary driving force to ensure victory. The first of the above *AV.* charms was employed in women's rites to appease anger (*Kauś.* 36,28–30). As the bow-string is removed from the bow, thus releasing the tension, so anger is removed from the heart of the person to be placated. Anger, regarded as an entity distinct from the person experiencing it,[4] is placed symbolically under a heavy stone which, when trampled on, sinks into the earth. The ritual prescribes that a person desiring to appease the wrath of another, should pick up a stone, replace it on the ground, spit on it, and finally lay an arrow on a bow whilst standing in the angry person's shadow, so symbolically destroying the rage because whatever falls or is placed on the ground loses much of its power. Thus, according to the Old Testament, Yahweh favoured Samuel and prevented any of his words 'falling to the ground' (I Sam. 3:19). The ancient Greeks held that whatever fell to earth belonged to the ancestral spirits, while some Germans today assign such objects to the devil.[5] The second charm relies on the magical powers of a *darbha* grass amulet, here called the 'appeaser of wrath' (*manyuśamana*). This grass is much lauded and employed frequently in ritual (*AV.* XIX.32 and 33); it is many-rooted and 'reaches down to the sea' – perhaps an allusion to the archaic belief that the earth floats on water.

To gain influence in the village assembly the suppliant addresses the meeting-place (*sabhā*) and the gathering (*samiti*), both being personified as the daughters of Prajāpati, who will aid him to gain the influence and understanding of the members present and make them agree with him. The Assembly is sometimes called *nariṣṭā* (merriment), which refers to the social side of the *sabhā* as distinct from the political. The *RV.* X.34,6 mentions that the meeting-place was also used for gaming; and in some cases for hostile practices (*AV.* V.31,6). The *sabhā* somewhat resembles the Homeric public meeting-places where people gathered to talk and exchange views, but which were also used as council halls.

The war-god Indra and the twin Aśvins were invoked for aid to overcome strife and bloodshed and to restore peace (*AV.* VII.52); it was hoped that Indra would bring peace by quickly conquering his suppliants' enemies, and that the Aśvins, as agricultural divinities, would ensure good harvests. The worshipper prays that Indra's arrow shall not be allowed to fall, 'the day being come', possibly an allusion to the first day of battle, when the war-god Indra shoots the first arrow. Thus 'not to let the arrow fall' means the prevention of bloodshed.

The horse sacrifice (*aśvamedha*) ritual included a prayer for harmony addressed to particular gods, as well as to the king, the commoners, the chariot and its horses, and finally to all creatures (*Tait. Saṁ.* VII. 5,23).

Many of the social and political problems of ancient India, though relatively limited, are fundamentally similar to those of medieval and modern India. The early examples are particularly interesting because they are the basis of much of the folklore of India and constitute an important part of its long cultural history.

Glossary

abhicakṣaṇa Conjuring; incantation.
abhicāra Exorcizing; employment of spells for a malevolent purpose; magic, one of the Upapātakas or minor crimes.
abhicāraka Enchanting, exorcizing; a magician.
abhicāra-mantra A formula or prayer for working a charm; an incantation.
ābhicārika Spell; enchantment; magic.
abhicaraṇīya Fit for enchanting or exorcizing.
adbhuta Portent.
Aditi An ancient Vedic goddess who personifies boundless space or infinity. She is the mother of the gods. Her nature is manifested 'in any expansion of phenomenal life' (Gonda, *Viṣṇuism and Śivaism*, p. 7).
Āditya(s) The sons of Aditi. They personify particular aspects of nature. The twelve Ādityas represent the twelve months of the solar year, and are sun-gods; *see* Sūrya.
ādri or *grāvan* 'Stone'. The pressing-stones used ritually to extract the *soma* juice.
aghamarṣaṇa The 'sin-effacing' *sūkta* (*RV.* X.190) still used by brahmins as a daily prayer. When recited it expiates wrong-doing and other evils.
Agni Fire as an element and its personification as the god Agni, the supreme life-principle. The carrier of the oblations to the gods. The three sacrificial fires are the *gārhapatya*, *āhavanīya* and *dakṣiṇā*.
Āhavanīya *see* Agni.
Airāvata Indra's four-tusked white elephant, a post-Vedic conception.
ajanani 'Non-birth', 'cessation of existence'. A term often used

in cursing an enemy, such as 'May he cease to exist!'

ajaśṛṅgī 'Having a goat's horn'. The shrub (*Odina wodier*) whose fruit resembles a goat's horn. It was used against demons by the ancient Atharvans.

ājya Melted or clarified butter (*ghee*) used for oblations, or for anointing anything sacrificed; it may also mean oil or milk oblations.

akṣa A die. Early dice consisted of small *vibhītaka* nuts; later oblong dice were used.

Alakṣmī or Aśrī 'Misfortune', 'bad luck', personified as the sister of Lakṣmī (or Śrī) the goddess of good fortune.

amīva Pain, grief, sickness.

Amīvā(fem.) Terror, fright, distress personified.

Amīva-cātana Driving away diseases or demons.

amṛta 'Immortal', 'imperishable'. Ambrosia, the nectar of immortality.

Aṁśa 'Apportioner'. One of the sons of Aditi. He represents luck in gaining wealth or booty.

aṅgavidyā The science of prognostication from the movements of limbs, gait, and the lucky and unlucky marks on the body.

Aṅgir Name of a *ṛṣi* who received the *brahmavidyā* from Atharvan and imparted it to Satyavāha, the teacher of Aṅgiras.

Aṅgiras A famous *ṛṣi* and fire-priest regarded as the first sacrificer and referred to by other *ṛṣis* as their 'ancient father'. The author of the *sūktas* of *RV.* IX, of a code of laws and of a treatise on astronomy.

Āṅgirasas The descendants of Aṅgiras or of Agni.

āñjana An eye-ointment from the Himālaya which gives protection against demons and spells.

annastuti Praise of food (*anna*).

antarikṣa The firmament, the intermediate region between earth and sky – the atmosphere.

Anumati(I) 'Divine favour' or 'approbation' personified as a goddess of the same name who bestows wealth, offspring and longevity on her worshippers.

Anumati(II) The goddess of the fifteenth day of the moon's age, on which it rises one digit less than full. On this day the gods receive oblations with favour.

Āpa or Āpas Water as element.

Āpadeva Name of the god (*deva*) of water (*āpa*), i.e., Varuṇa.
apāmārga The plant (*Achyranthes aspera*) common all over India. It is frequently used in incantations, medicine, and in sacrifices.
Apsaras (pl. Apsarasas) A class of seductive female divinities sometimes called nymphs. They are the wives of the Gandharvas and inhabit the sky, but often visit the earth. They are closely connected with gambling especially dicing. They can change their shapes at will.
Apvā Possibly the personification of a kind of colic caused by fear and experienced by warriors in battle.
araṇi The fire-drill. The process of making fire is likened to procreation.
Araru Name of a four-footed demon.
Arāti 'Meanness', 'envy', personified as a goddess of the same name.
Arāyī(s) One-eyed lame demonesses who destroy embryos.
Arbuda The serpent adversary of Indra. Perhaps the same as the serpent-demon Arbudi.
Arbudi *see* Arbuda.
Arthaśāstra Treatise on political science attributed to Kauṭilya.
arundhatī A plant used to heal bleeding from wounds.
Aryaman One of the sons of Aditi, who regulates the external performance of rituals, and also controls marriage contracts. The Milky Way is called his path.
Āryāvarta A part of northern India dominated by the Aryans in the second millennium BC.
āśis Prayer or wish.
aśman(I) 'Stone', i.e. Indra's weapon also called *vajra*.
aśman(II) In Vedic times the firmament was regarded as an inverted stone bowl.
aśna 'Voracious'. An epithet applied to one of the many demons overcome by Indra.
Asunīta 'Lord of spirits', i.e., Yama, the ruler of the dead.
asura 'Spiritual, incorporeal, divine'; a good or supreme spirit (said of Varuṇa). It also means 'lord' and 'demon', the latter meaning being predominant from the late Vedic period onwards. In the oldest parts of the Veda it is applied to the chief gods, thus *asura* and *deva* are sometimes used synonymously to signify divine beings possessed of creative vitality. Later it signified the demonic enemies of the gods.

asuramāyā Demoniacal magic.
asuravidyā The science (*vidyā*) of the *asuras*, i.e., magic or demonology.
Āsurī(I) A demoness, the discoverer of a remedy for leprosy.
āsurī(II) The plant *Sinapsis ramosa*. Perhaps Āsurī(I) personifies the plant.
Āśvalāyana Name of a pupil of Śaunaka's. The author of ritual works relating to the *RV*. and founder of a Vedic school.
Aśvin(s) 'Possessed of horses'. The name of twin divinities who appear in the sky before dawn. Their Avestan counterparts are the Aspinas. The Aśvins were credited with healing powers. Being themselves for ever young, they bestow longevity on their worshippers, as well as bringing treasures to them.
Atharvan The first priest to generate fire, to institute its worship and to offer *soma*. He is called the 'father of Agni' (fire). The authorship of the *AV*. is attributed to him. He is regarded as the eldest son of Brahmā who taught him the *brahmavidyā*.
Atharvāṇa The *Atharvaveda* or its ritual.
Atharvāṇas The descendants of Atharvan, often coupled with the descendants of Aṅgiras and Bhṛgu.
Atharvaveda The fourth of the four *Vedas*. *see Veda*.
Atri An ancient *ṛṣi* and sacrificer; author of some Vedic *sūktas* and a code of law; also the *purohita* of the Five Tribes, the earliest Aryan settlers in India. He is included among the Prajāpatis, the progenitors of mankind.
avakā An aquatic plant with sharp sword-like leaves, which represents water and moisture and is used in rites to prevent fire.
avatāra Lit. 'descent'. An incarnation of a deity.
Avesta The sacred writings attributed to Zoroaster (c. 1000 BC), the Iranian religious teacher. They consist of the *Vendidād*, the *Yasna* (including the *Gāthās* 'hymns' whose language is very close to that of the *RV*.), the *Yašts* ('hymns' of praise), and some other works.
Āyu 'Life or vitality' personified.
āyudhapuruṣa A weapon (*āyudha*) represented anthropomorphically. The *āyudhapuruṣas* have a role in ritual and in rites for protection.
Āyurveda The *veda* (science or knowledge) of *āyus* (life, health,

longevity). The *Āyurveda* is a traditional and naturalistic system of medical knowledge which in its early stages depended on the use of water, herbs, minerals and formic acid from ant-hills, for the cure of disease. Later the *Āyurveda* contributed to the development of chemistry by propounding a theory of chemical combination and division and classification of substances.

āyuṣyam 'Bestowing longevity'.

Babhru The 'tawny one'. An epithet applied to the *soma* beverage. It is also the name of a Vedic *ṛṣi* who mixed *soma* for Indra.

baja A herb, probably white mustard. An amulet of *baja* expels the demons from between the thighs of pregnant women.

bakura A horn, trumpet or other wind instrument used to rally troops. It provides the 'music of war', and terrifies enemies.

Bālagraha 'Seizer of children'. A malevolent spirit which causes nine kinds of demonic possession.

balbaja A coarse grass (*Eleusine indica*) said to be produced from the urine of cows. Sometimes used for the sacrificial seat (*barhis*) of the gods.

bāṇa 'Arrow'. The *RV.* refers to lightning as the 'lofty arrow', and also to the 'arrow of disease and death'. Arrows also have phallic significance.

bāṇaparṇī A poisonous plant used in sorcery.

barhis *see balbaja.*

Bhaga An Āditya, son of the cosmic mother-goddess Aditi. He gives man his share of happiness and thus embodies good fortune.

Bhaṅgā Hemp (*Cannabis indica*), a narcotic drug. *Bhaṅgā* is one of the 'five kingdoms of plants' ruled by Soma (the moon).

Bharadvāja A member of an ancient Aryan pastoralist tribal group of the same name.

Bhārgava A descendant of Bhṛgu.

Bhava One of the eight elemental forms of Rudra. Bhava is lord of cattle and of men. He is often associated with Śarva in destroying evil-doers and sorcerers.

Bhṛgu(s) A family of fire-priests who were initially taught the use of fire-sticks by the semi-divine Mātariśvan.

bhūta A malignant spirit, goblin or ghost.

bhūtavidyā 'Knowledge of spirits', i.e., demonology.

Bhūti 'Well-being', 'prosperity'. A name of the goddess of good fortune Lakṣmī.

bhūtonmāda Insanity, produced by the influence of *bhūtas*.

Brahmā The impersonal universal spirit (*brahman*) manifested as the active Creator of the universe Brahmā, the first god of the Hindu triad (*trimūrti*).

brahmacakra 'Brahmā's Wheel', i.e., the universe; also the name of a particular magic circle.

brahmacārin A religious student or pupil.

brahmagāyatrī A magical mantra modelled on the *gāyatrī* mantra.

Brahman(I) Pious utterance, prayer; a sacred text or mantra used as a spell.

Brahman(II) The universal Supreme Principle without attribute or quality.

Brāhmaṇa(s)(I) A class of works containing rules for the employment of mantras in connexion with various sacrifices.

brāhmaṇa(s) (II) A man (generally a priest) belonging to the first of the three 'twice-born' classes.

Brahmaṇaspati or Bṛhaspati The lord of prayer and spells; the *purohita* of the gods; the creator of the gods and of the priestly class (*brāhmaṇa*).

brahmapāśa Brahmā's noose – a mythical weapon.

brahmāstra 'Brahmā's missile'. A magical weapon which never fails to destroy the enemy.

brahmavidyā The essential sacred knowledge (*vidyā*) which Brahmā transmitted to his eldest son Atharvan from whom it was successively passed down to various sages including Aṅgiras.

bṛhacchānti The 'great [formulas] for averting evil'.

Bṛhaddevatā Name of a work giving the names of the deities to which each *sūkta* of the *RV*. is addressed.

Bṛhaspati or Brahmaṇaspati 'Lord of Prayer'. The chief offerer of prayers and sacrifices and therefore represented as typifying the priestly order.

cakra Discus, circle or ring; sharp-edged circular weapon; wheel of a chariot or wagon. A symbol of the sun, and of a *cakravartin*.

cakravartin A universal ruler.

cakṣur-mantra 'Bewitching with eye', i.e. the Evil Eye.

Caraka One of the three most important figures in the practice of Indian medicine (*āyurveda*). The others are Suśruta and Vāgbhaṭa.

cāraṇa(s) Celestial singers.
caru An oblation consisting of rice, barley and pulse boiled with butter and milk.
cāṣa The blue jay to whom disease was sometimes transferred.
cātana 'Driving away'. The name of a *ṛṣi* who instituted the use of the *cātana* verses of the *AV.* for exorcizing demons.
cātanāni 'Expellers', particularly those *sūktas* or verses of *sūktas* used for exorcism.
Cyavana Name of an ancient *ṛṣi* whose youth was restored by the Aśvins.
dadhi Thick sour milk used as a remedy for particular ailments.
Dakṣa A son of Brahmā. Dakṣa embodies ritual skill.
dakṣiṇā Donation or gift given by the institutor of a sacrifice to the priestly officiants. The *dakṣiṇā* is personified as a goddess who represents the female power of the sacrifice.
dakṣiṇa Right; south.
Dakṣiṇāgni The 'southern fire'. One of the three fires to which offerings are made. Dangerous powers are contained in this fire which is dedicated to the demons who dwell in the south (*dakṣiṇa*) – the sphere of death. The deceased are cremated in the *dakṣiṇāgni*.
Dakṣiṇapati 'Lord of the South'. An epithet of Yama, ruler of the dead.
dānastuti Praise of liberality.
dāsa(s) or *dasyu(s)* Epithets applied to the non-Aryan inhabitants of India who were finally overcome by the Aryans. It may also mean demon, enemy of the gods, barbarian, unbeliever, etc.
dasyu *see dāsa(s).*
deva or *devatā* A deity, celestial power.
devī (Feminine of *deva*). General name for any goddess.
Dhanvantari The divine physician of the gods.
dhāraṇā 'Concentration'; one-pointed concentration 'from *dhṛ* to hold'.
dharma Moral and religious duty, law, custom, order.
dharmapāśa The magical noose by which Varuṇa effortlessly controls and binds demons.
Dharmarāja 'King of Justice'. An epithet of Yama as the embodiment of law (*dharma*).
Dhātar (Vedic), Dhātṛ (Skt.) 'Establisher', 'arranger', 'supporter'. An Āditya associated with conception and who

also gives wealth, longevity, immortality and rain to ensure fertility.

Dhiṣaṇā A goddess of abundance and wife of the gods.

dhṛṣṭa A magical formula uttered over weapons.

Diti Goddess of earthly phenomena, the opposite of Aditi, goddess of boundless space.

Dṛṣṭidoṣa The Evil Eye.

druh A male or female member of a group of demons opposed to Indra. Cf. Avestan druj; German *trügen*.

duḥsvapna A bad dream. Such dreams were greatly feared.

dundubhi War-drum.

dundhubhisvana 'Drum-sound'. A mantra or charm used against the malevolent spirits believed to possess weapons.

dūrvā A marshland grass (*Cynodon dactylon*). A substitute for *soma*. It is efficacious against curses.

Dvita An Āptya. A vague mythological figure who, with Ekata and Trita, transferred the guilt of the gods to various evil-doers.

Dyaus The personification of the sky. Dyaus and Pṛthivī (the earth-goddess) are the parents of gods and of mankind.

edhas 'Fuel'. The sacred wood used for the sacrificial fire. It is invoked for prosperity, and is a pun on the roots *idh* 'burn' and *edh* 'prosper'.

ekacakra One (*eka*) wheel (*cakra*). A reference to the one wheel of the Sun's chariot drawn by seven horses.

ekākṣara The one imperishable (*akṣara*) mantra *OM* which overcomes all difficulties.

Ekāṣṭakā A goddess personifying the eighth day after the full moon who is invoked for children and longevity. She is the wife of the personified Year.

Ekata *see* Dvita.

ekoddiṣṭa Post-Vedic funerary rite performed after the cremation of a man to ensure union with his ancestors (*pitṛs*).

enas Sin, evil, misfortune.

gadā Mace or club. A weapon used in Vedic warfare. Favourite maces, as well as other weapons, were personified and named; *see* Āyudhapuruṣa.

gaja Elephant.

gandharva(s) Celestial beings, skilled in music and medicine, who dwell in the atmosphere. They attend the banquets of the gods and guard the sacred *soma*. The *AV*. describes them as shaggy, semi-human beings, having an earthy odour; sometimes they are depicted as handsome, rather effeminate men. The chief gandharva Viśvāvasu has a peculiar mystical power over women and hence is invoked in marriage ceremonies. Ecstatic states of mind and possession by evil spirits are caused by him.

Gaṇeśa The elephant-headed god of wisdom.

gārhapatya The householder's fire. One of the three sacred fires. It is the family or domestic fire transmitted by a father to his descendants thus linking each generation with the ancestors (*pitṛs*) and the gods. From it the sacrificial fires are lighted.

gāyatrī Also called *sāvitrī*. Initially a Vedic invocation of the sun being verse 10 of *RV*. III.62. It is repeated by brahmins at their daily morning and evening devotions.

ghee *see ghṛta.*

ghoṣiṇī(*s*) Female attendants of Rudra.

ghṛta Clarified butter (*ghee*), identified with *soma*. Because of its fatty nature it symbolizes prosperity. Fertilizing rain is regarded as the fat which drops from heaven. *Ghṛta* is also used medicinally.

Gñā(s) Vedic goddesses who probably belonged to the vegetal and fertility cults of non-Aryan India.

go Cow, bull. When the cow became identified with the life-giving and life-sustaining Vedic mother-goddess Aditi, its paramount importance was established. It represents all that is good; its five products are used in purificatory ceremonies.

gokarīṣam Dried cow-dung, sometimes used in rites to remove evil spirits.

graha 'Seizer'. A class of demons who 'seize' or 'possess' their victims. The Vedic demoness (Grāhi) causes wasting diseases especially among children.

grahāpasmāra 'Hysteria' believed to be caused by the baleful effects of particular stars and planets.

gṛhastha Householder. A 'twice-born' man who, after his period of studentship, performs the duties of the master of the house, father of the family, and as an economically productive member of society.

Gṛhya-sūtra A ritual work containing directions for domestic rites and ceremonies.

guggulu *Bdellium*, an aromatic gum-resin used in perfumes and medicines, and against curses.

guṇa Quality, property, characteristic. The three qualities or tendencies of which all creation is constituted – *sattva* (pure, ascending); *tamas* (obscure, inert, descending); *rajas* (active, expanding).

Gungū A Vedic lunar goddess.

haṁsa Goose. The Bar-headed goose (*Anser indicus*) which breeds on the lakes of Central Asia. In winter it migrates to every part of India. It is associated with the sun and represents purity and spiritual striving; also the male principle of fertility.

haridrā Turmeric (*Curcuma longa*). An aromatic plant of the ginger family, especially used for internal and cutaneous diseases such as leprosy. According to folk-belief, *haridrā* is much feared by demons.

hāridrava The yellow wagtail to whom jaundice was transferred from the human sufferer.

hariṇa 'Gazelle'. The horns were used in rites against the disease called *kṣetriya*.

haritala A yellowish-green pigeon to whom jaundice was transferred; *see hāridrava*.

havis An oblation or burnt offering.

hiṁsakarman An injurious act, especially by means of spells and atharvanic mantras.

homa The act of making an oblation to the gods by casting clarified butter (*ghṛta*) into the sacrificial fire.

hotrā A ritual call or invocation personified.

Hrūḍu or Hrūḍru Name of the god of fever (Takman).

iḍā or *iḷā* Sacrificial food or a libation consisting of four preparations of milk and personified as the cow, the symbol of food and nourishment. Iḍā is called the 'mother of the herds of cattle', i.e., of animals intended for sacrifice. Her place is at the northern altar, the place of libation, prayer and worship.

Ilībiśa A demon destroyed by Indra.

Indra The war-god of the Indo-Aryans, the embodiment of the strength and power of the heroic warrior, and the god of clouds and rain.

Indrajāla The net of Indra. In Vedic warfare nets were used to entangle the enemy. Later *indrajāla* meant the art of magic, sorcery.

Indrāṇī Indra's consort. She, like Indra, personified tremendous power.

Indra-Pūṣan The gods Indra and Pūṣan conjoined and invoked to give assistance in battle.

Indra-Soma Indra and Soma conjoined and invoked to perform heroic deeds for man, to give them strength, and to destroy demons and other enemies.

Indra-Varuṇa Indra and Varuṇa conjoined representing heroic and kingly power.

indu 'Drop'. An epithet of *soma* whose glorious drops give immortality and freedom from disease.

iṅgiḍa A plant or substance used in witchcraft rites.

itarajana 'Other folk'. A euphemism for secret spirits or *yakṣas*.

jaṅgiḍa A tree whose wood is used to make amulets to protect men and animals.

japa A muttered or whispered prayer; rhythmic repetition of a mantra, generally a text included in the *saṁhitās*.

Jātavedas 'Knowing [or known by] all created beings'. An epithet of Agni, god of fire.

jñāna Knowledge, especially spiritual knowledge and wisdom; insight gained by meditation.

Jvara Fever and its personification; *see* Takman.

Kalki or Kalkin The future incarnation (*avatāra*) of Viṣṇu.

Kāma The god of love.

kaṇva(s) Disease demons who devour embryos.

kapota A dove or pigeon. A bird of ill-omen.

kārīrīṣṭi A rain-spell.

Kasarṇīla Name of a snake killed by the white horse Paidva.

Kaśyapa A Vedic sage. Amulets and charms associated with him are peculiarly powerful.

Kauśika An ancient teacher, identified with Viśvāmitra, one of the seven great *ṛṣis*. The seventy-two *Atharvavedapariśiṣṭas* are attributed to him.

Kauśika Sūtra One of the two *sūtras* attached to the *AV*., the other being the *Vaitāna*.

kavya An 'inspired utterance'; 'a magically potent spell'.

khadira A hard wood from which sacrificial posts and ladles are made; its heart wood is used for amulets and the points of ploughshares.

kimīdin(s) Demons who are especially dangerous to pregnant women; they devour embryos and can change male embryos into female ones.

kṛmi Worm. Many diseases of men and cattle were thought to be caused by worms.

Kṛtyā Spell, enchantment, witchcraft, personified as a goddess (*abhicāradevatā*), to whom sacrifices are offered for destructive and magical purposes.

kṣetriya Some kind of incurable (or hereditary?) disease. According to the *AV*. the antidote is the horn of a gazelle (*hariṇa*).

kūdī A plant. Small bundles of its twigs were tied to the foot of a corpse so that its way to the realm of the dead would be obliterated, thus preventing its return to the living.

kumbha Pot-pitcher, or jar. These water-vessels are identified with mother-goddesses and represent the womb, the 'generative pot'.

Kuṇāru The 'handless' (or 'having a withered arm') demon crushed to death by Indra.

kuśa A sacred grass (*Desmostachya bipinnata*) commonly called *darbha* which possesses supernatural properties.

kuṣṭha An aromatic plant (*Costus speciosus* or *arabicus*) having great curative powers; also worn as an amulet.

Kutsa A Vedic mythical hero who with Indra defeated Śuṣṇa (the eclipse demon) and rescued the sun.

lākṣā A climbing plant used medicinally to cure wounds.

lakṣaṇa(*s*) Marks or signs. Some bodily marks were regarded as demonic, others were good; *see* Lakṣmī.

Lakṣmī or Śrī The Vedic mother-goddess personifying good fortune, happiness and beauty. In Vedic times *lakṣmī* also signified a mark or sign which could be good or bad, such as the English good or bad luck.

madhu Honey, regarded by the Vedic physician as the essence of all plant life and thus the possessor of fertilizing and life-giving properties.

madugha A species of plant yielding a honey-like substance used in making love-spells.

mahāśānti An expiatory rite for averting evil.

mālā A necklace, wreath or garland, believed to possess protective powers.

manas-pāpman 'Evil' regarded as an entity capable of entering into a man or woman.

maṇḍūka 'Frog' frequently employed in rain-spells.

maṇi A magic pearl or jewel used as an amulet; name of a collection of magical formulas.

mantra A sacred text or syllable, prayer or song of praise. A magical formula (sometimes personified), an incantation, invocation of a divinity, charm, spell or Vedic 'hymn'. In some witchcraft rites ceremonies are modified and mantras recited in inverted order as in the European Black Mass.

mantrin A knower of mantras; a wise man.

Manu-smṛti or *Mānava Dharma-śāstra* The Code or Institutes of Manu, a collection of laws based on custom and the teaching of the Vedas.

Manyu Wrath, fury, rage, personified.

māraṇa 'Killing', 'death' (*māra*). A magical ceremony intended to destroy enemies.

marmāṇi Mortal, vulnerable, or vital spots. In magical rites spells were placed in various objects such as a seat, drum, garment, etc. This is derived from the belief that a man is vulnerable both in his own body and through his belongings.

Marut(s) Storm-gods, the friends and allies of Indra.

Mātariśvan A divine being (or culture hero) who taught man the use of fire-sticks.

Maṭmaṭa(s) Pot-testicled demons having feet with the toes and heels reversed. They are especially dangerous to pregnant women.

mātṛ(*s*) or *mātṛkā*(*s*) (I) Particular diagrams written in characters to which a magical power is ascribed.

mātṛ(*s*) or *mātṛkā*(*s*)(II) Divine mothers connected with the waters, the earth, and with the sun-god as the male activating agent. The epithet *mātṛtama* 'very motherly' is applied to rivers.

māyā Witchcraft, magic, illusion. In the older texts it refers to an incomprehensible wisdom, supernatural power or wonderful skill. In the *AV.* it means magic or enchantment.

mekhalā A girdle or belt believed to bestow strength, power, and other benefits on the wearer.

mithuna A pair; couple of lovers. A pair of anything is believed to give increased power and potency.

Mitra A Vedic god, the 'friend' of man.

mohanī A magical charm employed to confuse an enemy.

Mṛtyu 'Death' and its personification.

mṛtyupāśa The noose (*pāśa*) with which Death (Mṛtyu) ensnares his victims.

muñja A tall hollow-stemmed grass (*Saccharum muñja*) used for purificatory purposes.

nāga(*s*) m. *nāgī*(*s*) f. Mythical snake-divinities living in great splendour in the nether worlds.

Nairṛta Belonging, or consecrated, to the goddess Nirṛti.

nākulī The 'ichneumon plant' (*Salmalia malabarica*) said to provide the ichneumon with an antidote to snake venom.

nāma Name; essence as distinct from form (*rūpa*). The repetition of a divine name ensures liberation (*mokṣa*), and bestows creative power.

Nārada An ancient seer.

nimba A tree (*Azadirachta indica*) used for exorcizing demons and for purificatory purposes. Its bitter fruit and leaves are chewed during funeral ceremonies.

Nirṛti Dissolution, destruction, calamity, evil and corruption personified as the goddess Nirṛti.

nirṛti(s) Destructive powers or potencies.

Nirukta Explanation or etymological interpretation of a word. The name of a commentary on the *Nighaṇṭu* by Yāska.

nyagrodha The Indian fig-tree (*Ficus indica*). Sacrificial bowls are made from its wood. Gandharvas and other godlings dwell in it.

nyāsa An ancient rite of fixing or assigning powerful formulas or mantras to various parts of the body, so associating them with their particular tutelary deities for purposes of meditation.

odana An oblation usually consisting of grain, or rice cooked in milk. It is closely associated with thaumaturgy and is said to possess the power of saving the oblation offerer from death.

Oṃ The most sacred mantra, the 'seed' of all mantras, uttered at the beginning and end of a reading of the Vedas, or preceding any prayer. Since Upaniṣadic times onwards Oṃ is an object of the deepest religious meditation. Supreme spiritual efficacy is attributed to it.

oṣadhi A plant or herb, especially a medicinal one.

Oṣadhipati 'Lord of herbs'. An epithet of the Moon and the title of a physician, i.e. 'Master of herbs'.

padma Lotus, especially the flower of the *Nelumbium speciosum* which symbolizes purity and spiritual striving.

pañcagavya The five (*pañca*) products of the cow, namely, milk, sour milk, butter, urine and dung.

Papī lakṣmī Personification of bad luck as a goddess.

Parjanya The god of rain, a son of Dyaus, the sky.

parṇa (later *palāśa*) The tree (*Butea monosperma*) whose leaves are used for sacred purposes, its wood for making amulets for victory, wealth and longevity.

pāśa Noose, snare or fetter.

pāṭā A medicinal climbing plant used in spells to remove rivals and overcome hostile disputants.

Pathyā The 'Auspicious Path' personified as a goddess of happiness and welfare.

Paurṇamāsī A goddess personifying the night of the full moon.

Pedu A royal *ṛṣi* and protégé of the Aśvins who gave him the snake-killing white horse Paidva (belonging to Pedu).

Piṅga A godling invoked to protect a baby during the actual process of birth and to ensure that it is male.

piśāca(s) Flesh-eating demons.

plakṣa One of the trees in which Gandharvas and Apsarasas dwell.

pradakṣiṇa Ceremonious circumambulation of sacred objects, shrines, etc., from left to right, performed as an act of respect, submission, devotion, or sacrifice.

Prajāpati 'Lord of creatures', progenitor. Originally an epithet applied to several Vedic gods and then applied to one god. The Brāhmaṇas equate Prajāpati with Brahmā.

pramatha(s) 'Tormentor'. A class of demons or sprites belonging to ancient Indian folklore. When depicted on the lower portion of temple doorways they exert an auspicious influence.

prāṇa 'Breath of life', 'life-principle'.

prāṇāyāma Name of three breath exercises associated with yogic techniques of controlling breathing. It includes exhalation (*recaka*), inhalation (*pūraka*) and suspension (*kumbhaka*) of breathing.

pṛśniparṇī The plant (*Hemionitis cordifolia*) having a spotted leaf which wards off Kaṇva who causes miscarriages. The plant is personified as a goddess of the same name.

Pṛthivī The Earth and its personification as a goddess.

priyaṅgu An auspicious fragrant medicinal plant from which perfumes are also made. It is frequently used in religious ceremonies.

puṁsavana A rite to ensure the birth of a male child.

Puraṃdara 'Destroyer of Castles', an epithet of Indra.

purāṇa Ancient stories describing creation and destruction of the world, the feats of gods, *ṛṣis*, heroes, etc.

Puraṃdhi A Vedic goddess personifying abundance and liberality.

purohita A specially gifted priest, a kind of 'chaplain' to a king, who was capable of averting evil influences and counteracting witchcraft.

Puruṣa The Supreme Being or Essence of the universe; the personal and animating principle in man. The spiritual principle as distinct from *prakṛti*, the material substratum of creation.

Pūṣan Protector of cattle and of human possessions in general; the knower and the guardian of paths and ways.

pūtika also called *ādāra* A plant used as a substitute for the *soma* plant.

rājasūya A Vedic rite, the inauguration of a king.

Rākā A goddess associated with childbirth and the bestowal of prosperity.

rakṣā Any amulet, bracelet, or token used as a charm (from the root *rakṣ* 'to guard').

rakṣāmaṇi A jewel (*maṇi*) worn as an amulet.

rākṣasa(s) Malignant demons (*rakṣas*) who roam about at night. They haunt burial grounds, disturb sacrifices, etc. They can assume many forms including men, birds and animals.

rakṣāsarṣapa Mustard used as a protection against evil spirits.

Rakṣohan Killer of demons (*rakṣa(s)*) – an epithet of Agni; see *rākṣasa(s)*.

Rātrī 'Night' personified as a goddess.

ṛc. Sacred verse recited in praise of a deity.

Ṛgveda The 'Veda of praise', the first and most important of the four Vedas. A repository of sacred lore consisting of a collection (*saṁhitā*) of so-called 'hymns' (*sūktas*), composed of verses (*ṛcs*). The nucleus of the *RV.* dates from c. 1500 BC, but contains earlier material.

Ṛgvidhāna A work containing many magical and devotional practices, some of which are non-brahmanic, but all are integrated and validated by citations from the Vedas.

ripra Dirt, pollution, impurity. No distinction was made between pollution, sin, and curses.

Rohiṇī Consort of the rising sun Rohita. Rohiṇī is the divinity of cattle.

Rohita 'Red'. A name of the sun-god.

ropaṇāka A bird to which disease is transmitted from a human patient.

ṛṣi A singer of sacred *sūktas*; an inspired poet or sage. The Vedas were revealed to the seven ancient *ṛṣis* at the beginning of time.

Ṛta The fundamental principle of law, order, truth, duty, etc.

Rudra Vedic god of the tempest who was greatly feared. He became in post-Vedic times the God Śiva ('Auspicious'). The term *śiva* was initially an epithet of Rudra which finally became a separate deity.

śabara mantra(s) Obscure formulas of unknown meaning, still used in some magical rites.

Śacī Also called Indrāṇī or Aindrī. A goddess who, like her consort Indra, personifies divine power.

sadaṁpuṣpa 'Ever-flowing'. A herb from which amulets are made. It enables the wearer to detect, and thus avoid, sorcerers.

sadāṇvā(s) A class of demonesses who inhabit the foundations of houses.

sādhya(s) A class of celestial beings who may personify the rites of the *Vedas*. They dwell above the realm of the gods.

sahasrākṣa 'Thousand-eyed', i.e. 'all-perceiving'. An epithet of Agni and of an amulet made of *varaṇa* wood, said to ward off malignant influences.

śakuna Any omen or portent derived from the movements of particular auspicious birds.

Śakunādhiṣṭātrī The goddess presiding over good omens.

śakunajñāna Divination by the movements of birds and omens.

śālmali The silk-cotton tree (*Salmalia malabarica*) much used medicinally, and for making bridal carriages.

sāman(s) Songs of praise chanted as part of sacrificial ritual.

Sāmaveda One of the four *Vedas*. The *Veda* of sacred songs (*sāmans*), consisting mostly of verses taken from the *Ṛgveda* and modified to suit liturgical requirements.

śamī A hard wood tree (*Prosopis spicigera* or perhaps *Acacia suma*), said to contain fire and thus it was used for the fire-drill (*araṇi*) to kindle the altar fire.

saṃjñānam Harmony or unanimity.

sāṃnipātika A rite performed immediately a sudden or unexpected event occurs.

śaṅkha General name for sea-shells, particularly the conch-shell variety. Used as ornaments, amulets, trumpets to rally troops in battle, and later as libation vessels.

śānti Any expiatory or propitiatory rite for preventing the adverse effects of disease; of curses, of adverse stellar influences, and thus giving tranquillity and peace.

śapatha or *śapana* Curse or imprecation.

Saramā The 'fleet one'. The name of Indra's messenger or watchdog, and the dam of Yama's two dogs who guard the road to the realm of the dead.

Sārameya(s) The metronymic of the two dogs of Indra's bitch Saramā, who roam the road to the realm of the dead.

Sarasvatī A goddess personifying an ancient river of the same name (not the modern Sarasvatī river). As a river-goddess she is connected with fertility, procreation, and especially with purification. When identified with Vāc, goddess of speech and learning, she is the tutelary deity of writers and poets, and wife of Brahmā.

sarpa or *nāga* Snake.

Śarva 'Archer'. The name of one of the eight elemental forms of the god Rudra who later was incorporated in the composite deity Śiva.

Saṣṭhī A folk-goddess, regarded as a form of Durgā. She personifies the sixth day after the birth of a child, when the child's destiny is fixed. The cat is sacred to her.

Savitar A name of the sun-god Sūrya.

Sāvitrī *see* Gāyatrī.

Sāyaṇa A famous fourteenth-century commentator on the *Ṛgveda* and the author of numerous works.

shamanism The indigenous religion of the Ural-Altaic peoples of northern Asia and Europe, from Lapland in the West to the Bering Straits in the East. The term shamanism is also loosely applied to the religions of the North American Indians, Eskimos, and the inhabitants of Oceania, because shamanistic elements are prominent in these religions. To a certain extent shamanistic elements can be seen also in the higher religions.

Shamanism presupposes a belief in countless spirits, some malevolent and some benevolent to man, and in a continued life after death for the individual soul.

The shaman (a word derived from the Tungusian *šamān* meaning 'priest' or 'medicine man') is a person capable of mediating between the world of spirits and man. His most important ritual instruments are the drum and staff. By drumming he summons his spirit-helpers; with the staff he treats the sick, and also conducts the souls of the dead to the next world. (Cf. the magical staffs of Moses and Aaron.) Beyond the spirits are the supreme deities such as the High God of the Evenks of Siberia.

siddhārthaka 'White mustard'. The word is derived from *siddhārtha* meaning 'successful' and is efficacious against demons.

Sinīvālī A lunar goddess who personifies the new moon. She appears in the form of a crescent in the headdress of Śiva. Sinīvālī helps to fashion the embryo in the womb, and is also associated with cattle and conducts them safely to their byres.

Sītā A furrow or track of a ploughshare personified as a goddess of the same name. In the *Ṛgveda* she presides over agriculture and the fruits of the earth. She is Indra's wife; in epic poetry the wife of Rāmacandra.

Śiva Lit. 'Auspicious'. Name of one of the two great gods of Hinduism and the focus of worship in the Śaiva cult. In the form of Rudra he was present in Vedic religion.

śmasāna sādhana Magical rites performed in cremation grounds to gain control over malevolent spirits.

śodhanamantra A purificatory mantra.

soma The beverage of the gods. The name of the most important Vedic plant and its personification as a god. The juice pressed from it was the most important ingredient in Vedic sacrifices. Its hallucinogenic properties made people who drank it experience such extraordinary feelings and visions that they were convinced it was of divine origin. It bestows wealth, longevity, and vanquishes death.

śrāddha Ceremony performed for the benefit of dead ancestors, on special occasions. Three or any other odd number of brahmins represent the ancestors.

śrauṣat A ritual exclamation when making a sacrificial offering. Other ritual calls were *vaṣat*, *svāhā* and *svadhā* – all believed to be magically potent.

Śrī The goddess of good fortune; *see* Lakṣmī.

śruti The eternally sacred words or texts 'seen' or 'heard' by certain *ṛṣis*.

stuti Praise; *see* Āśis.

sudarśana A discus or wheel (*cakra*). An emblem of Viṣṇu.

Sudarśana is sometimes personified and depicted as a small man; *see āyudhapuruṣa* and *cakra*.

śuka Parrot. The diseases of human beings were sometimes transferred to parrots or other birds, and also to animals.

sūkta *Su – ukta*, well or properly said or recited; a wise saying; a 'prayer-hymn' or song of praise; an invocation.

Śunāsīra The personification of plough and ploughshare as the dual agricultural deities Śuna and Sīra. Plough-shaped amulets were worn.

surā Intoxicating liquor personified as a goddess (Surādevī).

Sūrya or Savitar The name of the Vedic sun-god who incorporates a number of other solar deities. He possesses curative powers, and represents immortal life which the dead will attain when they ascend from earth to him. He is the centre of creation, the point where the manifested and unmanifested worlds unite. Sūrya is the chief Āditya of the seven (or eight) sun-gods called Ādityas.

Sūryā Daughter of the sun-god Sūrya.

Sūṣaṇā A goddess invoked to ensure easy parturition by 'loosening' the womb.

Suśruta saṁhitā A medical work compiled by Suśruta, reputed to be a son of Dhanvantari, the physician of the gods; *see Āyurveda*.

Svadhā *see śrauṣat*; *svāhā*.

svāhā One of a number of ritual exclamations used when making oblations. Each offering must be presented with a mantra consisting of the name of the divinity in the dative case; *see śrauṣat*.

Svasti-devī Goddess (*devī*) of the home and giver of prosperity. She may be identical with Pathyā-svasti, the goddess personifying the prosperous way or path.

svastyayana Blessing, benediction, welfare – a spell or mantra to obtain the above blessings, etc.

Takman (later jvara) Fever and its personification.

tapas 'Warmth', 'heat', 'asceticism'. The last is also called *ugra* 'austere, mighty'. By the practice of *tapas* one can attain and accumulate supranormal powers including overcoming death.

tarpaṇa 'Satiating' or 'refreshing' the gods and the deceased by libations of water, etc.

tārpya A garment made from vegetable fibre used in funerary rites. It is also associated with ritual rebirth.

tejas Fiery energy, spirit, vital power, lustre, majesty, etc.

Trita or Trita Āptya The Vedic counterpart of the Avestan deity Thrita. Trita is sometimes regarded as a double of Indra.

Tvaṣṭṛ or Tvaṣṭar The divine craftsman, the creator of all forms, invoked by those desiring offspring.

ucchiṣṭa 'Residue', 'remnant', especially the remains of sacrificial offerings which have great ritual significance. Aditi had sons by eating the remains of food she had cooked for the Sādhya gods.

udumbara A tree (*Ficus glomerata*) from which sacrificial articles are made as well as a variety of amulets.

ulūka Owl. A bird of ill-omen.

Upaniṣad *see Veda.*

utpāta Any unexpected event or portent, particularly a calamity. Man's collective wrong-doing accumulates and forms an actual entity which upsets the course of nature.

Vaitaraṇī The foetid river which flows between the earth and the realm of the dead.

vājapeya The 'drink of strength', a rite which ensures victory.

vajra The magical weapon of Indra, the Aryan war-god.

varada(s) The Benefactors, a particular class of deceased ancestors who grant wishes.

varaṇa The tree (*Crataeva Roxburghii*) from which amulets are made.

Varuṇa One of the oldest Vedic gods, originally a personification of the sky. The ruler of the physical and moral world and custodian of *ṛta* (law and order). He afflicts evil-doers with dropsy.

vaṣaṭ or *vauṣaṭ* See *śrausat.*

vaśīkaraṇa The act of bewitching anyone by means of spells.

Vāstoṣpati 'Protector of the house'. A divinity who presides over the foundations of a house.

Vāstupuruṣa The archetype design of a house personified as a divinity.

vāstuśamana A rite performed to pacify spirits living on the intended site of a house, the building of which would otherwise arouse their hostility.

vaṭa The Indian fig-tree (*Ficus indica*). In Vedic times its juice was the drink of kings, as *soma* was that of priests.

Veda Lit. '[Divine] knowledge' revealed by Brahmā to the *ṛṣis*. Initially there were three *Vedas*, the *Ṛg*, *Yajus* and *Sāma*, to which later the *AV.* was added. Included in the *Veda* are the *Brāhmaṇas* (treatises on the sacrificial ritual), and the *Upaniṣads* (metaphysical speculations on the ultimate Truth). Together they constitute the basis of the Hindu religion and metaphysics.

vedi Altar.

Vendidād *see Avesta.*

vibhītaka A tree (*Terminalia bellerica*) employed in maleficent rites. Dice are made from its nuts.

vidveṣa A magical act or formula for exciting hatred.

Viliptī The mysterious divine cow which the gods caused to rise from the sacrifice.

viṣa Poison.

Viṣṇu One of the two great gods of Hinduism, the other being Śiva. Viṣṇu has a number of incarnations (*avatāras*).

viṣṭārin A particular kind of cooked rice-offering. It enables the sacrificer to overcome both death and enemies.

Viśvāmitra A famous Vedic sage and reputed author of many of the *sūktas* of *RV.* III, including the *gāyatrī*, and also some *AV. sūktas.*

Viśvadeva 'All-divine'. A particular class of deities (Viśvedevāḥ).

Vṛtra The demonized power of obstruction vanquished by Indra.

vyāhṛti(s) The mystical utterances of the names of the seven worlds; the 'great *vyāhṛtis*' are the names of the first three worlds – *bhūr, bhuvaḥ, svaḥ* – which are pronounced by brahmans after the sacred mantra Oṃ at the commencement of their daily prayers.

yajamāna A sacrificer, or institutor of a sacrifice (*yajña*). The offerings made in this world are said to constitute his body in the next, so freeing him from mortality and 'sin'.

Yajurveda One of the four *Vedas.*

yajña 'Oblation', 'sacrifice', offered to the gods. The sacrifice, as in all religions, is essentially magical.

Yakṣa(s) Vegetal godlings of rural India. Their worship goes back to pre-Vedic days. Formerly Yakṣa was the designation of the world-creator, equivalent to Puruṣa or Prajāpati.

Yakṣma The personification of disease.

Yama The ruler of the dead, and later the Judge of the Dead.

He was the first man to die; he conducts the dead to his realm (Yamaloka).

Yāska The patronymic of the author of the *Nirukta* (a commentary on the difficult Vedic words contained in the lists called *Nighaṇṭus*).

yātu or *yātudhāna* A fiend or demon who sometimes resides in the vicinity of large stones. *Yātu* also means witchcraft or sorcery.

yava Any grain yielding flour or meal. In the *AV*. it usually refers to barley.

yāvaka A food prepared from barley (*yava*), used in a *yāvaka-kṛcchra*, a penance consisting in eating the above food for a week, fortnight, or month.

yūpa A post, pillar or beam, especially a sacrificial post to which the victim was attached.

Zoroaster The teacher of the religious system contained in the *Avesta*. Zoroastrianism flourished in Persia until overthrown by Islam in the seventh century.

Notes

Introduction

1 S. K. Chatterji, 'Race Movements and Prehistoric Culture', in *The History and Culture of the Indian People,* ed. R. C. Majumdar, I, Allen & Unwin, 1951, p. 154.

2 The earliest designation of the *AV.* was Atharvāṅgirāsaḥ, i.e. the formulas and rites of the Atharvāṇas and Aṅgirasas, the two hereditary classes of fire-priests or fire-churners', who were subsequently joined by Bhṛgu, ancestor of the priestly Bhārgavas. Later names of the *AV.* were *Brahmaveda* and *Bhṛguvistara.*

3 *A History of Indian Literature*, I, pt i, p. 111; see also Hoernle, *Studies in the Medicine of Ancient India*, pt i, p. 9.

4 S. Wikander, *Feuerpriester in Kleinasien und Iran*, pp. 12ff.

5 H. R. Zimmer, *Hindu Medicine*, p. 29.

6 As late as the latter half of the twentieth century, Roman Catholic, Anglican and African clerics are much concerned with the problems of black magic, demonic possession and exorcism.

7 The later Hindu household ceremonies are also connected with fire, whereas the greater Vedic rites centred on oblations of soma.

8 In the ritual texts the adjective āṅgirasa is equated with ābhicārika, 'sorcerer'; saṁbhara āṅgirasaḥ means 'utensils for sorcery'; daṇḍa āṅgirasaḥ, a 'staff for sorcery'; agnir āṅgirasaḥ, 'sorcery-fire'; āṅgirasaḥ, 'witchcraft charms'.

9 Cf. the modern form of exorcism advocated by the members of the Commission convened by the Bishop of Exeter in 1972: 'I command you, every unclean Spirit, in the Name of God the

Father Almighty, in the name of Jesus Christ his Son. . .' (*Exorcism*, ed. Dom Robert Petitpierre, OSB, 1975, p. 45). Father J. H. Crehan, SJ, also a member of the Commission, writes: 'if one were to conclude that the existence or non-existence of the devil did not matter to the salvation of mankind, then it would be pertinent to ask what really does matter to that end' (p. 12). For further information concerning 'name', see M. and J. Stutley, *A Dictionary of Hinduism,* under Nāman.

10 J. Filliozat, in *The Encyclopaedia of Buddhism*, ed. G. P. Malalasekera, Government of Ceylon, 1961, p. 477.

1 Medical charms

1 René Dubos, *Man, Medicine and Environment*, pp. 161f.
2 S. N. Kramer, *History Begins at Sumer*, p. 103.
3 Zimmer points out that European alchemy and kindred esoteric teachings were formed along the same pattern of thought as that which engendered the Hindu concept of the *doṣas* (*Hindu Medicine,* pp. 13f.).
4 A. F. Anisimov, 'The Shaman's Tent of the Evenks and the Origin of the Shamanistic Rite', in *Studies in Siberian Shamanism*, ed. H. N. Michael, p. 101.
5 Cf. the Biblical passage referring to the Lord visiting 'the iniquity of the fathers upon the children, upon the third and upon the fourth generation' (Num. 14:18).
6 In European medicine fever is a symptom of a number of diseases, but in ancient medicine it was regarded as a disease in itself.
7 See R. F. G. Müller, 'Der Takman des Atharvaveda', pp. 230–42.
8 M. Eliade, *Occultism, Witchcraft and Cultural Fashions*, p. 105.
9 H. Zimmer, *Hindu Medicine*, p. 133.
10 Rawlinson, *Inscriptions of Western Asia*, ii, 51b, 11, 1ff.
11 H. Zimmer, *Myths and Symbols in Indian Art and Civilization*, p. 34.
12 *The Forbidden Books of the Original New Testament of Jesus Christ*, Ch. 19, verses 20f., translated by Archbishop Wake *et al.*
13 R. L. Turner, *A Comparative Dictionary of the Indo-Aryan Languages*, 3370, 3371, 1966.
14 See also Burrows, *JRAS*, 1973, p. 138, n. 31.
15 Lucy Mair, *Witchcraft*, p. 65.
16 R. C. Thompson, *The Devils and Evil Spirits of Babylonia*, II, p. 133.

17 An evil-smelling plant (*Guilandina bonduc*). Cf. the Sanskrit *pūtika* meaning putrid.

18 Perhaps *ulapa* – the grass *Saccharum cylindricum* (Turner, op. cit., 2357).

19 *Muñja* grass is often used in charms probably because of its connexion with the idea of 'loosening', since disease was thought of as a 'binding' agent. Also *muñja* puns with *munka*, 'release'.

20 Thompson, op. cit., II, Intro., p. xxxviii; for other examples of disease-transference see his *Semitic Magic*, pp. 165f., 212f.

21 Ye. D. Prokofyeva, 'The costume of an Enets Shaman', in *Studies in Siberian Shamanism*, ed. H. N. Michael, pp. 152f.

22 H. Sigerist, *A History of Medicine*, II, pp. 67f.

23 H. Zimmer, *Hindu Medicine*, p. 4.

24 A. Boissier, *Choix de textes*, vol. II, pp. 235ff.

25 Paul Ghalioungui, *Magic and Medical Science in Ancient Egypt*, p. 35; for transference of disease in ancient Egypt see Georges Posener (ed.), *A Dictionary of Egyptian Civilization*, p. 156, English translation 1962.

26 Eric Stone, *Medicine among the American Indians*, p. 79.

27 Pedro Laín Entralgo, *The Therapy of the Word in Classical Antiquity*, p. 21.

28 Cf. the Biblical story of Yahweh punishing Miriam with leprosy (Num. 13:10). In some ancient cultures skin diseases were said to be punishments for lying or violating taboos; thus in ancient Egypt anyone who drank the milk of a sow was certain to get leprosy.

29 *Āsurī* is also the name of a 'magical' (healing) plant, perhaps mustard (*Sinapsis ramosa*) (Turner, op. cit., 1496). Probably herbal lore was in the hands of particular women who handed it on to their daughters.

30 Gaster, *The Oldest Stories in the World*, p. 94.

31 R. Caminos, *Late Egyptian Miscellanies*, p. 197. Cf. the German reference to toothache – es wurmt mich – 'the worm has got me!' Cf. also the Sanskrit *kṛmidantaka* – 'caries'. In East Prussia whitlow is called 'Nagelwurm'.

32 Brough, *The Early Brahmanical System of Gotra and Pravara*, p. 19. Cf. Isa. 30:27f. where the Name of the Lord is said to come from afar, burning with anger and with thick rising smoke. The ancient Greeks, even when the forefather of their clan was known, would take the name of a great man from the primeval past 'in order to throw the origin of the family as far back into

the past as possible and connect it the more closely with a divine source' (Erwin Rohde, *Psyche*, p. 125).

33 This is the large, tall wood-apple tree whose leaves and flowers have a strong odour of anise. The young leaves are given to children suffering from bowel complaints.

34 The eagle is probably the fabulous Vedic bird Garutmant (later called Garuḍa), the declared enemy of all snakes. (See Stutley, *A Dictionary of Hinduism*, under Garuḍa and Kadrū.)

35 Gaster, *Thespis*, p. 304 and n. In Europe today bee stings are considered by many to have medicinal properties; also the so-called Royal Jelly derived from bees which is sold as a beauty preparation.

36 *ERE*, VIII, p. 251.

37 *Hindu Medicine*, p. 36.

38 Cf. the ash-altar Ge at Olympia which was believed to be 'charged with the presence of the divinity' (Farnell, *The Cults of the Greek States*, vol. IV, p. 221, note c).

39 Zimmer, *Hindu Medicine*, p. 43.

40 *Nirukta* 6,30 describes them as 'ever-screaming'. One named *Arāyī* is a one-eyed, limping, screeching hag (*RV*. X.155,1).

41 A. Kuhn long ago pointed out a number of parallels with Teutonic, Norwegian and English charms, including that of Wotan curing the sprained leg of Baldur's foal: 'Bone to bone, blood to blood, limb to limb, as if they were glued'.

42 Thompson, *Devils and Evil Spirits of Babylonia*, II, pp. 109ff.; E. A. W. Budge, *Egyptian Magic*, pp. 137ff.

43 F. L. Cross (ed.), *The Oxford Dictionary of the Christian Church*, p. 126.

44 Radford, *Encyclopaedia of Superstitions*, p. 319.

45 Or 'she that takes root'. The masculine form is the name of one of the personified bricks of the fire-altar (*Tait. Saṁ*. IV.4.5,1).

46 E. S. Drower, *The Mandaeans of Iraq and Iran*, p. 118, n.2. Psychologists recognize that the excessive washing of hands by some patients indicates a desire to remove or 'wash away' hidden feelings of guilt.

47 P. Ghalioungui, *Magic and Medical Science in Ancient Egypt*, p. 142; G. Posener (ed.), *A Dictionary of Egyptian Civilization*, p. 164.

48 Bloomfield suggests boils or tumours. Rudra has the epithet Jalāṣabheṣaja 'whose remedy is jālāṣa' (*RV*. I.43,4; *AV*. II.27.6).

49 *Vedische Studien*, 3, 139, n. 2.

50 J. Aubrey, Royal Society Ms., folio, 168.
51 Böhtlingk and Roth, *Sanskrit Wörterbuch*. Apacit is from the root *ci – apa* 'pick off'. Cf. Latin scabere; German die Schabe, schaben; English, scab.
52 Cf. the Greek myth of Otos and Ephialtes who, to fight the immortal gods, piled Ossa on Olympos and Pelion on Ossa. They were destroyed by Apollo.
53 *Bdellium* is mentioned in the Bible (Gen. 2:12; Num. 11:7).
54 Jurgen Thorwald, *Science and Secrets of Early Medicine*, p. 197.
55 Th. Gaster, *Thespis*, p. 32. Another example is the Mazdean demon Ariš who was 'conjured up from an innocent adverb' (R. C. Zaehner, *Zurvan*, p. 149. For other Hindu ritual exclamations see Stutley, *A Dictionary of Hinduism*, under vaṣat; śrauṣat; svāhā and svadhā.

2 Charms for longevity

1 Weston la Barre, *The Ghost Dance*, p. 200. The ancient Egyptians regarded gold as the flesh of the gods. Gold conferred divine survival, giving to the Pharaohs the eternal life of the gods (G. Posener (ed.), *A Dictionary of Egyptian Civilization*, p. 111).
2 See Gonda, *Eye and Gaze in the Veda*, p. 42.
3 Cf. the ancient Christian method of invoking the Holy Spirit in exorcist techniques by a deep exhalation over the 'possessed' person, a method still practised in the Roman Catholic Church. See *Exorcism*, ed. Dom Robert Petitpierre, 1975, p. 21.
4 *Myth, Legend and Custom in the Old Testament*, vol. I, p. 19.
5 H. Zimmer, *Hindu Medicine*, p. 120.
6 Ibid., p. 123.
7 Gaster, *The Holy and the Profane*, pp. 161ff. For further parallels see his *Myth, Legend and Custom in the Old Testament*, vol. I, pp. 19f.
8 Erica Reiner, *Šurpu*, p. 11.
9 See Coomaraswamy, *Yakṣas*, pt 1, p. 32. In ancient times the girdle had wide significance both as a sacrificial ornament and as an amulet. Cf. Aphrodite's girdle which contained the enchantment of love (*Odyssey*, xiv.215).
10 These two dogs and their dam Saramā may be the prototypes of the Greek three-headed dog Cerberus who also guards the way to the place of the dead.

3 Charms relating mainly to women

1 R. C. Majumdar (ed.), *History and Culture of the Indian People*, Allen & Unwin, 1951, I, p. 389.
2 In Tantric cults copper is associated with blood, life and fertility, and probably has the same significance in this ritual.
3 Kāma, the Indian god of love, has arrows, as does Cupid. Pliny states that sleeping on arrows extracted from a victim acts as a love-charm.
4 Kāma originally meant creative force, but later became equated with sexual desire.
5 Cf. the use of the thumb in the common European anti-demonic device in the gesture called 'to fig' – the Italian *far la fica*, German *die Feige weisen*, French *faire la figue* and the Spanish *hacer el higo*. This was, and is, an insulting gesture and is meant to be an obscene representation of the sexual act.
6 Figuratively honey means sweetness or charm and hence is a word of endearment especially in the USA. Cf. also the term honeymoon.
7 Cf. the bean tabu observed by Orphics, Pythagoreans and by Empedocles.
8 In the Vedic view procreation was equivalent to the performance of a sacrifice, a worship of god (*Chāndogya Upaniṣad* V.8).
9 A special rite was performed if a birth occurred at an inauspicious time.
10 *Exorcism*, ed. Dom Robert Petitpierre, OSB, 1975, p. 21.
11 The ancient Indo-Iranian demon of purpureal fever,*Ala, often attacked the newly-delivered infant and the mother (E. Benveniste, 'Le dieu Ohrmazd et le demon Albasti', pp. 65–74). In Aryan tradition the witch and lying-in woman were almost one and the same; the death of a woman in childbirth was regarded as magically dangerous (J. J. Meyer, *Sexual Life in Ancient India*, p. 393n.).
12 M. Boyce, *A History of Zoroastrianism*, vol. I, p. 56.
13 R. L. Turner, *A Comparative Dictionary of the Indo-Aryan Languages*, p. 780, col.2.Cf. Susani, the name of an accouching goddess.
14 Grose, *Dictionary of the Vulgar Tongue*.
15 Hillebrandt, *Ritualliteratur*, §14.
16 White and yellow mustard may have been fashioned into an

amulet; perhaps in the form of a doll composed of mustard plants and which reached from the neck to the navel of the pregnant woman to protect her (Whitney, *The Atharva-Veda Saṁhitā*, vol. II, p. 494n.).

17 J. J. Meyer, op. cit., p. 393n.

18 For other rites performed during pregnancy, see V. Henry, *La magie dans l'Inde antique*, pp. 81, 138, 144.

19 Meyer, op. cit., p. 437 and n.4.

4 Charms pertaining to royalty

1 Langdon, *Semitic Mythology*, p. 206; A. R. Johnson, *Sacral Kingship in Ancient Israel*, p. 14.

2 Montgomery, *Journal of Biblical Literature*, 1909, vol. 28, p. 59.

3 The name is derived from bṛh 'prayer' and pati 'lord'. Edgerton (*The Beginnings of Indian Philosophy*, p.20, n.1) points out that both Bṛhaspati and Brahmaṇaspati are purely ritualistic deities in the older *RV. sūktas*. This is borne out by the purohita being called the king's 'ritual father' (Heesterman, *Ancient Indian Royal Consecration*, p. 56, n.40). The performance of a sacrifice produces much greater effects than the causal act itself because of the supernatural effect of prayer. The Zoroastrians also appreciated the power of prayer which they personified as the god Sraoša whose epithet was tanu mąthra, 'having the sacred word for body'.

4 The *parṇa* tree was so highly regarded that its wood was used for the making of sacrificial utensils, and for sacrificial posts (*yūpa*).

5 Dumézil suggests that Varuṇa and Mitra are opposite aspects of 'sovereignty' (*Numen*, vol. 8, 1961, published by the International Review of the History of Religions, Amsterdan, pp. 36ff.). The ancient Irish personified the 'sovereignty of Ireland' as a beautiful goddess. The Egyptian Pharaohs were obliged to husband their resources for the welfare of the cosmos. The jubilee festival was performed for this purpose at the end of thirty years' rule and thereafter 'at short intervals. . .The ceremony allowed the king to renew his vital force and to be his own successor' (Georges Posener (ed.), *A Dictionary of Egyptian Civilization*, pp. 212f.).

6 J. Auboyer, *Le trône et son symbolisme dans l'Inde ancienne*, pp. 175ff.

7 Heesterman, op. cit., p. 109.

8 See Hocart, *Kingship*, pp. 83f.; I. Engnell, *Studies in Divine Kingship in the Ancient Near East*, p. 5.

9 The bull is also connected with royal ideology in ancient Egypt it being identical with the king and thus 'a substitute for him. This is corroborated not only by the east and west Semitic material but also by that from all the relevant African cultures' (Engnell, op. cit., p. 200, n.5). For the symbolism of the 'centre of the world', see Eliade, *Images and Symbols*, pp. 27ff.

10 H. R. Ellis Davidson, 'The smith and the goddess' in *Fruhmittelalterliche Studien*, 3 (1969), p. 222.

11 For other spells pertaining to royalty, see W. Caland, *Altindisches Zauberritual*, pp. 37ff.

12 Mary Boyce, *A History of Zoroastrianism*, vol. I, pp. 67f.; and see John Irwin, 'Aśokan Pillars: a reassessment of the evidence (pt iv) Symbolism' *Burlington Magazine*, London, vol. cxxviii (November 1976), pp. 748ff.

13 The commentator Sāyaṇa considers it was in the 'form of an army'. Either interpretation would make sense in this context as the couch would symbolize the peaceful possession of the kingdom; the army, its conquest by force.

5 Battle charms

1 *Saṁgrāma* means 'assembly', either in peace or war. In the latter event it means an 'armed band'; in the *AV.* and later texts it refers to 'war' or 'battle'.

2 *Mohanāni* from *moha*, 'loss of consciousness', 'bewilderment', 'distraction', etc. Cf. the demonic Mohanī the Deluder and Enchantress, and *mohanāstra* – one of the five arrows of the god of love, Kāma, which stupifies and fascinates those against whom it is directed.

3 A number of *cakras* and other Indian weapons are exhibited in the Pitt Rivers Museum, Oxford.

4 For descriptions of weapons, etc., see S. D. Singh, *Ancient Indian Warfare with Special References to the Vedic Period.*

5 Magical powers exist in the war-drum itself and are inherent in the rhythm of its sound, as in the 'medicated' drum which cures snake-bite (*Suś. Saṁ.* II.pp. 737f.). In India thunder is called the 'drums of heaven'. The Yakuts and Buryats have a drum called the 'Shaman's horse' by which the Shaman undertakes mystical journeys to 'regions inaccessible to mankind' (M. Eliade, *Shamanism*, p. 174. Cf. the folklore attaching to Drake's Drum in Buckland Abbey, Plymouth.

6 Brough, *The Early Brahmanical System of Gotra and Pravara*, p. 2, defines *gotra* 'as an exogamous patrilineal sibship, whose members trace their descent back to a common ancestor'.
7 Cf. the importance of flags to American, European, African and other armies; also the blessing of flags and guns by Christian clerics; the placing of regimental flags in churches, etc.
8 *Origin and Influence of the Thoroughbred Horse*, pp. 153f.
9 *Soma, Divine Mushroom of Immortality*, and his *Soma and the Fly-agaric*; J. Brough, *BSOAS*, XXXIV, 1971, pp. 331–62; I. Gershevitch, 'An Iranist's View of the Soma Controversy', pp. 45–75.
10 J. Auboyer, *Daily Life in Ancient India*, p. 284.
11 Maxime Rodinson, *Mohammed*, pp. 166f.; Ibn Hishām, *Sīra, Das Leben Muhammeds*, ed. F. Wüstenfeld, p. 445, Göttingen, 1859–1860; see also Sale's translation of the *Koran*, surah iii.
12 'Saxo Grammaticus', tr. by O. Elton, *Journal of the Folklore Society*, London, 1894, p. 204.
13 Cf. the power attributed to the Hebrew sacrifice, and that stemming from the Crucifixion. In India, the correct performance of a sacrifice was believed to achieve whatever the sacrificer desired, even immortality.
14 Edited by E. W. Budge, 1904.
15 For further information see Stutley, *A Dictionary of Hinduism*, under Kṛtyā; J. J. Meyer, *Sexual Life in Ancient India*, pp. 241, n.1; 366n. The ancient Egyptians also personified magic as the god Ḥeka, who was known in the Old Kingdom (c. 2780–2280 BC) and later (Piankoff, 'Une statuette du Dieu Ḥeka', *Mélanges Maspero*, vol. I, 349ff.).
16 Similar methods were used by the ancient Egyptians who inscribed the names of nations or rulers they feared on figurines which were then trampled on, burnt or mutilated, so as to render harmless those they represented (Georges Posener, *A Dictionary of Egyptian Civilization*, p. 157).
17 *Tapas* also means 'austerity', 'asceticism', and is always associated with the notion of 'heat' and increased power, see Chauncey Blair, *Heat in the Ṛig Veda and Atharvaveda*.

6 Charms to protect priests and their possessions

1 The *dānastutis* (praises of gifts) referred to in the Vedic *sūktas* are either independent *sūktas* or stanzas at the end of *sūktas* lauding

the generosity of sacrificers to the priests. According to the *Śrauta Sūtras*, vast amounts of property and livestock were given as *dakṣiṇās*, and were doubtless intended to encourage future sacrificers to be liberal. The *Nirukta* I.7 derives *dakṣiṇā* from the root dakṣ 'to cause to accomplish', or from dāś 'to give'.

2 See also A. Hillebrandt, *Ritualliteratur*, pp. 140f.; S. Lévi, *La doctrine du sacrifice*, pp. 90f.

3 Cf. ME. mare 'incubus', German Alp or Mahre, Lithuanian maras 'death'.

4 A 'fee' includes cattle, property, money, etc. Cf. Latin *pecus*, the neuter form refers to cattle, money; peculium, property in the shape of cattle, private property; Skt. paśu, 'cattle', from root paś 'to fasten' or 'bind'.

5 M. Bloomfield, *Hymns of the Atharvaveda*, p. 656.

6 M. Douglas, *Purity and Danger*, p. 52.

7 Cf. the Old Testament statement that the firstborn of man and of clean and unclean beasts were the 'property' of Yahweh and had to be redeemed (Num. 18:15).

8 Cf. *ŚBr.* III.4.2,6 where the gods know the mind of man – his thoughts pass on to his breath, the breath to the wind, and the wind informs the gods.

9 Cf. *Vāj. Saṁ.* XXXV.13: 'For our well-being we hold on to the ox, sprung from Surabhi; even as Indra to the gods, so be thou a saving leader unto us!'

10 R. C. Thompson, *Semitic Magic*, p. 227.

11 See also M. and J. Stutley, *A Dictionary of Hinduism*, under 'Go' (cow).

12 *Hymns of the Atharvaveda*, p. 660.

13 According to the *ŚBr.* XI.3.3,1, the brahman delivers all creatures over to Death except the *brahmacārin*.

14 M. Douglas, op. cit., p. 142; Lucy Mair, *Witchcraft*, p. 40.

15 Other kinds of black magic are carried out in the funerary fire; sorcerers sometimes placed spells in the fire and also into human bones, but these spells can sometimes be 'hurled back' to the flesh-eating (funerary) fire (*AV.* V.31,9).

16 Richard Cavendish, *The Black Arts*, p. 327.

7 Charms and imprecations against demons, sorcerers and others

1 R. C. Thompson, *The Devils and Evil Spirits of Babylonia*, Preface, p. xii.

2 Sukumari Bhattacharji, *The Indian Theogony*, pp. 249, 254, 262f.

3 Richard Cavendish, *The Black Arts*, p. 326; Scott, *Outline of Modern Occultism*, p. 115.

4 *Catholic Encyclopaedia*, vol. IV, p. 277, cited by Cavendish, op. cit., p. 326.

5 *Ṛgvidhāna* I.15,4ff. translated by J. Gonda, Utrecht, 1951.

6 *Abhicāra* means 'exorcizing, incantation, employment of spells for maleficent purposes'; *abhicāra-mantra*, prayer or incantation for working a spell. *Yātu* is the term for demonic beings – some kindly, but the majority malignant, in Indo-Iranian traditions. Initially *yātu* denoted demons only, but later the term was applied to magicians and sorcerers who were capable of controlling the *yātus*. For further information on the Avestan and Indian *yātus* see F. Spiegel, *Die arische Periode und ihre Zustande*, pp. 218ff. and A. Christensen, *Essai sur la demonologie Iranienne*. Cf. *yātudhāna* which means an evil spirit, literally 'holding a demon'; *yātumat*, 'practising witchcraft or sorcery', 'malignant'.

7 Cf. *ŚBr.* XII.7.1,7 where Indra's life-breath is said to have flowed from his navel and become lead. This reflects the belief that lead is associated with the planet Saturn (*Śani*) which is the lord of death in Indian and European occultism.

8 Th. Gaster, *Myth, Legend and Custom in the Old Testament*, vol. II, p. 437. Samson's great strength resided in his hair which when shorn reduced him to a weakling.

9 J. Gonda suggests that this refers to a man who can achieve with his eyes the baleful effects which are usually caused by incantations (*Eye and Gaze in the Veda*, p. 39. Cf. the Babylonian Tablet III.1ff. of the *Maqlû* series: 'A witch has looked on me and pursued me with her venom. . .' The bridal veil originated as a protection against overlooking by the Evil Eye).

10 Una Maclean, *Magical Medicine*, p. 95. It is reported that the pseudo-Shamans among the Apaches of the Mescalero Indian Reservation in New Mexico who used the hallucinogenic peyote cactus (*Lophophora williamsii*) for illicit witchcraft purposes, found that the peyote 'turned back' on them, causing one to lose a leg in an accident, and the other to lose his nearest relatives (Boyer *et al.*, 'Shamanism and Peyote Use among the Apaches . . .', in *Hallucinogens and Shamanism*, ed. M. J. Harner, p. 57).

11 Power was believed to reside in the staffs of Shamans, in the rod of Moses and the blossoming rod of Aaron, in the wand of Hermes who guides the souls of the dead to the underworld, and in the wands of European magicians. In ancient Egypt amuletic wands were made of hippopotamus ivory incised with figures of minor deities. Both the ivory and the figures were believed to possess magical properties which could be invoked by rubbing the wand (J. Rawson, *Animals in Art*, illus. p. 50, British Museum, 1977).

12 But C. J. Blair, *Heat in the Ṛig Veda and Atharvaveda*, p. 117, considers that the verse means that 'whilst the funeral fire heats the body, may Heaven and Earth be heated (by the sun) against the ritual enemy'.

13 John Brough, *The Early Brahmanical System of Gotra and Pravara*, p. 17.

14 This is a common method of cursing such as 'may he cease to exist!' (*ajananị*); cf. the modern slang-term 'Drop dead!' The philosophical concept of 'non-being' (*a-sat*) is said to have risen from the earth for the express purpose of turning against the performer of spells. In other words the sorcerer is to be made 'non-existent'. The Assyrian fire-god was invoked to overcome sorcerers who have looked upon their victim 'as a corpse' (Thompson, *Semitic Magic*, p. 152).

15 Maclean, op. cit., p. 140.

16 E. Reiner, *Šurpu*, p. 11.

17 Tablet K. 249, published by Boissier, *Revue Sémitique*, II, 135, 1894.

18 E. Reiner, op. cit., pp. 11; 27f.

19 Erwin Rohde, *Psyche*, p. 295; Jane Harrison, *Prolegomena to the Study of Greek Religion*, p. 85.

20 *Kṛtyā* also means magic, personified as a female divinity, who is described as blue and red and clinging closely to her victim (*RV*. X.85,28f.); she is similar to the Assyrian demoness Ardat lilî, who attracted men and copulated with them as did the Greek Sirens and the European incubus or nightmare. According to some Indian Lexicons, sacrifices are offered to Kṛtyā for destructive and magical purposes. Thus *kṛtyakā* means 'enchantress' or 'witch', a woman who is the cause of injury or destruction; kṛtyakṛt, 'one who practises magic or sorcery'; *kukṛtya*, an evil deed (Turner, *A Comparative Dictionary of the Indo-Aryan Languages*, 3205). The *kṛtyā* resembles, in some respects, the *wanga* of Haitian Voodoo, an evil charm which is magically

conveyed to certain objects making them dangerous to those against whom the *wanga* is directed.

21 Cf. the custom, still practised in Haitian Voodoo, of convoking sorcerers by the loud clashing of stones, a signal also used by the Zangbeto – a secret society of Dahomey (A. Métraux, *Voodoo*, p. 294).

22 Cf. the ash-altar at Olympia which was 'charged with the presence of the divinity' (Farnell, *The Cults of the Greek States*, IV, p. 221, n.c.).

23 Cf. the contest between Elijah and the priests of Baal on Mount Carmel, when Elijah's magic proved more powerful than theirs and hc had them all slain (1 Kgs. 18:21ff.).

24 Métraux, op. cit., p. 285. Métraux also recounts a story concerning a twentieth-century historian who was at one time a member of the Conseil d'État. On his way to a reunion at the Presidential palace, he brought some seed for his pet birds, and put it in his brief case, which had a hole in it. As he crossed the assembly hall he left a trail of grain behind him. Immediately his alarmed colleagues shouted 'wanga, wanga!' The next day he was summoned by the President who said: 'My dear friend, I am too educated to believe in these silly tales of black magic, nevertheless I feel it my duty to ask you to resign!'

25 R. C. Thompson, op. cit., Preface, p. xiii.

26 For the ritual use of cow-dung see J. J. Meyer, *Trilogie*, II, pp. 50, 93f.

27 Métraux, op. cit., p. 274, citing M. Marcelin, 'Les Grands dieux du vaudou haitien', p. 122; *Journal de la Société des Americanistes de Paris*, n. ser., vol. 36, 1947.

28 Verse 22 also mentions owl, owlet, cuckoo, eagle and vulture-sorcerers – all probably familiars.

29 Betty Heimann, 'Hinduism', pp. 146f.

30 Maclean, op. cit., p. 32.

31 W. Sargant, *The Mind Possessed*, p. 122.

32 Gonda, *Eye and Gaze in the Veda*, p. 19. Cf. the power thought to reside in the Evil Eye.

8 Expiatory rites and charms

1 Bishop Atterbury, *Sermons*, I.2.

2 *A Dictionary of the Bible*, ed. James Hastings, vol. I, p. 812.

3 *ERE*, vol. V, p. 659.

4 G. S. Kirk, *Heraclitus. The Cosmic Fragments*, Intro., p. 5.

5 Cf. the Hebrew transference of sin 'even to the third and fourth generation'; according to Mic. (7:19), all our sins are to be cast into the sea; in Zechariah wickedness was sent to the land of Shinar.
6 Cf. Psalm 91:5. See Th. Gaster, *Myth, Legend and Custom in the Old Testament*, vol. II, p. 813.
7 Jean Wier, *Histoires, Disputes et Discours des Illusions et Impostures des Diables*, p. 284.
8 Cf. the fiction put about by some fox-hunters that the fox enjoys being hunted! Also the Wildfowlers who maintain that they are the 'real conservationists' (BBC2, 'Living on the Land', 22 August 1975).

9 Charms for prosperity

1 The *RV.* includes many prayers for wealth in the form of cattle. As early as Ṛgvedic times a verbal root gup, 'to protect' was evolved from the denominative go-pāya, 'to guard cows'. The Bhāratas were called the 'horde desiring cows'.
2 *Cows, Pigs, Wars and Witches*, pp. 19f.
3 R. C. Thompson, *Semitic Magic*, p. 227.
4 The Babylonians also had a god and goddess of the house who protected it against demonic beings, (R. C. Thompson, *The Devils and Evil Spirits of Babylonia*, vol. I, p. 177).
5 I. C. Peate, *Tradition and Folk Life. A Welsh View*, p. 32.
6 The Vedic bhūti and vibhūti originally signified great power and well-being (R. L. Turner, *A Comparative Dictionary of the Indo-Aryan Languages*, 9553), and later came to mean sacred ash which plays an important part in some Indian cults, especially Śaivism. Both Hindus and Moslems prize the ashes of sacred fires as prophylactics. For the evil-averting and fecundating power of ashes see Meyer, *Trilogie*, III, p. 288. For the ritual use of ash in Zoroastrianism see Mary Boyce, *A History of Zoroastrianism*, vol. I, p. 323.
7 F. R. Allchin, *Neolithic Cattle-Keepers of South India*, p. 178 and see 176; see also K. Paddayya, *Investigations into the Neolithic Culture of the Shorapur Doab, South India*, 1973. The *RV.*, VI.28,1, states that cattle were kept in pens. According to a Canaanite Ras Shamra text, the god El cured the sick King Krt by moulding an image of 'goodly dung' (*n'm rt*) into which the disease was transferred (John Gray, *The Legacy of Canaan*, Leiden, 1965, p. 150).
8 Could this be a reference to ancient 'cattle-rustling' and the

changing of marks or brands? The American cow-boy is often called a cow-puncher.

9 The *Nirukta*, 9,40 identifies them with Vāyu, the wind-god and the Āditya (sun); the *ŚBr.*, II.6.3,2, explains śuna as 'prosperity' and sīra (or sāra), 'sap' or 'essence'.

10 Cf. the marriage 'hymn' (*AV.* XIV.2) in which women are called a 'field wherein men sow', and the passage in the Koran (II:22): 'Your women are your plough-land'.

11 For ploughing rites see A. Hillebrandt, *Ritualliteratur*, p. 85; and J. J. Meyer, *Trilogie*, I, pp. 113ff.

12 The Maruts are said to make the reciters 'look thoroughly at the clouds', so that their eyes 'direct or transmit to them the power which is inherent in their words' (J. Gonda, *Eye and Gaze in the Veda*, p. 16).

13 *AV.* VII.18. Cf. the Canaanite Baal who contains the rain in great buckets as an act of imitative magic in the ritual. 'He opens a window in the house. A shutter in the midst of the palace. "Open, O Baal, the clouds with rain"' (Gordon, *Ugaritic Handbook*, 51, vii.25–8). Also cf. Job 38:37: 'Who can. . .tilt the bottles of heaven'. According to Teutonic mythology, rain was discharged by the gods from celestial bowls (Grimm, *Teutonic Mythology*, p. 593).

14 See Stuart Piggott, *Prehistoric India*, 1962 edn, pp. 268f.; R. A. Crossland, *Cambridge Ancient History*, 1971 edn, vol. I, pp. 873f. The light war-chariot was introduced into the Near East c. 1800 BC.

15 It is uncertain whether originally there were twenty-seven or twenty-eight constellations.

16 See also A. Hillebrandt, op. cit., p. 94.

10 Charms for harmony

1 Mary Boyce, *A History of Zoroastrianism*, p. 40, and her article, 'Varuṇa's part in Zoroastrianism', in *Mélanges E. Benveniste*, ed. M. Moīnfar, Paris, 1975, pp. 57ff.

2 An almost literal translation by Winternitz, *History of Indian Literature*, vol. I, pt i, pp. 121f.

3 *La religion romaine archaïque*, p. 205; and see Edgerton, *Beginnings of Indian Philosophy*, p. 115.

4 Accroding to the *Mahābhārata*, the ṛṣi Cyavana's wrath assumed the form of a large demon called Mada.

5 Th. Gaster, *Myth, Legend and Custom in the Old Testament*, p. 451; E. Rohde, *Psyche*, p. 245, n.1.

Bibliography

ALLCHIN, F. R., *Neolithic Cattle-Keepers of South India*, Cambridge University Press, 1963.

ALSTER, B., *The Instructions of Suruppak. A Sumerian Proverb Collection*, Copenhagen, 1974.

AUBOYER, J., *Le trône et son symbolisme dans l'Inde ancienne*, Paris, 1949.

AUBOYER, J., *Daily Life in Ancient India*, trans. S. M. Taylor, London, Weidenfeld & Nicolson, 1965.

AUTRAN, CHARLES, *L'Épopée indoue*, Paris, 1946.

BENVENISTE, E., 'Le dieu Ohrmazd et le demon Albasti', *JA*, 1960, pp. 65ff.

BERG, CHARLES, *The Unconscious Significance of Hair*, Allen & Unwin, 1951.

BHATTACHARJI, SUKUMARI, *The Indian Theogony*, Cambridge University Press, 1970.

BLAIR, CHAUNCEY J., *Heat in the Ṛig Veda and Atharvaveda*, AOS, vol. 45.

BLOOMFIELD, M., *Hymns of the Atharvaveda*, SBE, 1961, vol. 42, Oxford University Press, 1897; reprinted Delhi, 1964, 1967.

BLOOMFIELD, M., *The Atharvaveda and the Gopatha Brāhmaṇa*, Strasbourg, 1899.

BLOOMFIELD, M. (ed.), *The Kauśika Sūtra of Atharva Veda*, 1889, reprinted 1976.

BÖHTLINGK, O. VON and ROTH, R., *Sanskrit Wörterbuch nebst allen Nachträgen*, St Petersburg, 1855ff. Trans. into English by M. Mishra, ed. J. L. Shastri, 7 vols, 1973.

BONNER, C., *Studies in Magical Amulets*, University of Michigan Press, 1950.

BOYCE, MARY, *A History of Zoroastrianism*, vol. I: *The Early Period*, Leiden, 1975.

BREASTED, J. H., *The Edwin Smith Surgical Papyrus*, 2 vols, University of Chicago, 1930.

BROUGH, JOHN, *The Early Brahmanical System of Gotra and Pravara*, Cambridge University Press, 1953.

BROWN, W. NORMAN, 'Theories of Creation in the Rig-Veda', *JAOS*, vol. 85, 1965.

BUDGE, E. A. W., *Egyptian Magic*, reprinted Routledge & Kegan Paul, London, 1979.

BUDGE, E. A. W., *Paradise of the Fathers*, 1904.

BURLAND, C. A., *The Magical Arts*, Arthur Barker, London, 1966.

CALAND, WILLEM, *Altindisches Zauberritual*, Amsterdam, 1900, reprinted 1970.

CAMINOS, R., *Late Egyptian Miscellanies*, Oxford University Press, 1954.

CAVENDISH, RICHARD, *The Black Arts*, Routledge & Kegan Paul, London, 1967.

CHAKRABORTY, C., *Common Life in the Ṛgveda and Atharvaveda*, 1977.

CHRISTENSEN, A., *Essai sur la demonologie Iranienne*, Copenhagen, 1941.

CLEMENTS, F. E., *Primitive Concepts of Disease*, University of California Publications in American Archaeology and Ethnology, vol. 32, 1932.

COHEN, JOHN, *Chance, Skill and Luck*, Penguin, Harmondsworth, 1960.

COOMARASWAMY, A. K., *Yakṣas*, 2 vols, Smithsonian Misc. Collections, vol. 80, No. 6, Washington, 1928, 1931; reprinted 1971.

CROOKE, W., *Religion and Folklore of Northern India*, Oxford University Press, 1926.

CROSS, F. L. (ed.), *The Oxford Dictionary of the Christian Church*, 1966.

CROSSLAND, R. A., *Cambridge Ancient History*, 3rd edn, vol. I, 1971.

CROWLEY, ALEISTER, *Magick in Theory and Practice*, 1929; reprinted in *Magick*, Routledge & Kegan Paul, London, 1972.

DANIÉLOU, ALAIN, *Hindu Polytheism*, Routledge & Kegan Paul, London, 1963.

DAREMBERG, C. H. and SAGLIO, E. (eds), *Dictionnaire des antiquités grecques et romaines*, Paris, 1877–1919.

DAWSON, W. R., *Magician and Leech*, London, Methuen, 1929.

DOUGLAS, MARY, *Purity and Danger*, Penguin, Harmondsworth, reprinted 1970.

DROWER, E. S., *The ndaenMandaeans of iraq and Iran*, Leiden, 1962.

DUBOS, RENE, *Man, Medicine and Environment*, Penguin, Harmondsworth, 1970.

DUMÉZIL, GEORGES, *La religion romaine archaïque*, Paris, 1966.

DYMOCK, W., *Pharmacographia Indica*, 3 vols, Dehradun, 1976.
EDGERTON, F., 'The Philosophical Materials of the Atharvaveda', in *Studies in Honor of Maurice Bloomfield*, New Haven, 1920.
EDGERTON, F., *The Beginnings of Indian Philosophy*, Allen & Unwin, London, 1965.
EDGERTON, F., 'Dominant Ideas in the formation of Indian Culture', *JAOS*, vol. 62, 1942.
EDSMAN, C. M. (ed.), *Studies in Shamanism*, Stockholm, 1967.
ELIADE, MIRCEA, *Images and Symbols*, trans. by Philip Mairet, London, Harvill, 1961.
ELIADE, MIRCEA, *Occultism, Witchcraft and Cultural Fashions*, University of Chicago, 1976.
ELIADE, MIRCEA, *Shamanism: Archaic Techniques of Ecstasy*, Routledge & Kegan Paul, London, 1964.
ENGNELL, I., *Studies in Divine Kingship in the Ancient Near East*. Oxford University Press, 1967.
ENTRALGO, PEDRO LAÍN, *The Therapy of the Word in Classical Antiquity*, ed. and trans. by L. J. Rather and J. M. Sharp, New Haven, 1970.
FARNELL, L. R., *The Cults of the Greek States*, 5 vols, Oxford University Press, 1896–1909.
FILLIOZAT, JEAN, *Classical Doctrine of Indian Medicine*, Paris, 1949, trans. 1964, Luzac, London.
FILLIOZAT, JEAN, 'Pronostics médicaux akkadiens, grecs et indiens', *JA*, 1952.
FURST, PETER T. (ed.), *Flesh of the Gods: The Ritual Use of Hallucinogens*, New York, Praeger, 1972.
GASTER, TH., *The Oldest Stories in the World*, Boston, 1958.
GASTER, TH., *Thespis*, Harper & Row, New York, 1966.
GASTER, TH., *Myth, Legend and Custom in the Old Testament*, 2 vols, Harper & Row, New York, 1975.
GASTER, TH., *The Holy and the Profane*, Sloan, 1955.
GELDNER, K. F., and PISCHEL, R., *Vedische Studien*, 3 vols, Stuttgart, 1889–1901.
GELDNER, K. F., *Der Rig-Veda*, HOS, 3 vols, 1951 and Index 1957, reprinted 1971.
GERSHEVITCH, I., 'An Iranist's View of the Soma Controversy', *Mémorial Jean de Menasce*, ed. P. Gignoux, Paris, 1975.
GHALIOUNGUI, PAUL, *Magic and Medical Science in Ancient Egypt*, London, Hodder & Stoughton, 1963.
GONDA, J., *Eye and Gaze in the Veda*, Amsterdam, 1969.
GONDA, J. (trans.), *The Ṛgvidhāna*, Utrecht, 1951.

GONDA, J., *Les religions de l'Inde: Védisme et Hindouisme ancien*, Paris, 1962.

GONDA, J., 'The Indra Festival according to the Atharvavedins', *JAOS*, vol. 87, 1967.

GONDA, J., *Ancient Kingship from the Religious Point of View*, Leiden, 1969.

GONDA, J., *Die Religionen Indiens, I. Veda und älterer Hinduismus*, Stuttgart, 1960.

GONDA, J., *Viṣṇuism and Śivaism*, London, Athlone Press, 1970.

GRIFFITH, R. T. H. (trans.), *The Hymns of the Ṛgveda*, 2 vols, reprinted Varanasi, 1963.

GRIFFITH, R. T. H. (trans.), *The Texts of the White Yajurveda*, Benares, 1927.

GRIFFITH, R. T. H. (trans.), *The Hymns of the Sāmveda*, Varanasi, 1963.

GRIFFITH, R. T. H. (trans.), *The Hymns of the Atharvaveda*, 2 vols, reprinted Varanasi, 1968.

GROSE, F., *Dictionary of the Vulgar Tongue*, London, 1811; Northfield, Illinois, 1971.

HALLIDAY, W. R., *Indo-European Folk-Tales and Greek Legend*, Cambridge University Press, 1933.

HARNER, M. J. (ed.), *Hallucinogens and Shamanism*, New York, 1973.

HARRIS, MARVIN, *Cows, Pigs, Wars and Witches. The Riddles of Culture*, Hutchinson, London, 1975; reprinted 1977, Fontana.

HARRISON, JANE E., *Prolegomena to the Study of Greek Religion*, Cambridge University Press, 1922.

HARTMANN, FRANZ, *Magic White and Black*, Kegan Paul, 1893; reprinted 1969.

HASTINGS, JAMES (ed.), *A Dictionary of the Bible*, 5 vols, T. & T. Clark, Edinburgh, 1906.

HEESTERMAN, J. C., *Ancient Indian Royal Consecration*, The Hague, 1957.

HEIMANN, B., 'Hinduism', in *The Eleven Religions and Their Proverbial Lore. A Comparative Study* by S. G. Champion, London, Routledge, 1944.

HENRY, VICTOR, *Les livres VIII et IX de l'Atharva-Véda, traduits et commentés*, Paris, 1894.

HENRY, VICTOR, *Les livres X, XI et XII de l'Atharva-Véda, traduits et commentés*, Paris, 1896.

HENRY, VICTOR, *La magie dans l'Inde antique*, Paris, 1904.

HILLEBRANDT, A., *Vedische Mythologie*, 2nd edn, Breslau, 1927–9, 2 vols, reprinted 1965.

HILLEBRANDT, A., *Ritualliteratur*, Strasbourg, 1897, reprinted 1974.

HILTERBEITEL, A., *The Ritual of Battle. Krishna in the Mahābhārata*, ed. V. Turner, 1976.

HUBERT, A. M., *Kingship*, Oxford University Press, reprinted 1970.

HOERNLE, A. F., *Studies in the Medicine of Ancient India*, pt 1, Oxford University Press, 1907.

HUBERT, H. and MAUSS, M., 'Esquisse d'une théorie générale de la magie', *Mélanges d'histoire des religions*, Paris, 1909.

IRWIN, JOHN, '"Aśokan" Pillars: a reassessment of the evidence. Part iv. Symbolism', *Burlington Magazine*, vol. 128, November 1976, pp. 734–53, London.

JAHODA, G., *The Psychology of Superstition*, Penguin, Harmondsworth, 1971.

JAYNE, W. A., *The Healing Gods of Ancient Civilizations*, New Haven, 1925.

JOHNSON, A. R., *Sacral Kingship in Ancient Israel*, University of Wales, 1955.

JOLLY, J., *Indian Medicine*, trans. from German, reprinted 1977.

KEITH, A. B. (trans.), *Ṛgveda Brāhmaṇas: Aitareya and Kauṣītaki Brāhmaṇas of the Ṛgveda*, HOS, vol. 25, 1920, reprinted 1971.

KEITH, A. B., *The Veda of the Black Yajus School entitled Taittirīya Saṁhitā*, HOS, 2 vols, 1914, reprinted 1967.

KING, F., *Ritual Magic in England*, Spearman, London, 1970.

KIRK, G. S., *Heraclitus. The Cosmic Fragments*, Cambridge University Press, 1962.

KRAMER, S. N., *History Begins at Sumer*, Thames & Hudson, London, 1958.

KRAMRISCH, S., 'The Banner of Indra', *Essays in honour of A. K. Coomaraswamy*, ed. K. B. Iyer, London, 1947.

LA BARRE, WESTON, *The Ghost Dance*, Allen & Unwin, London, 1970.

LANGDON, S. H., *Semitic Mythology*, 1931.

LEACH, E. R., 'Magical Hair', *Journal of the Royal Anthropological Institute*, vol. 88, 1958.

LEVI, ELIPHAS, *Transcendental Magic*, reprinted 1968.

LÉVI, SYLVAIN, *La doctrine du sacrifice dans les Brāhmaṇas*, Paris, 1898; 2nd edn, 1966.

L'ORANGE, H. P., *Symbols of Cosmic Kingship in the Ancient World*, Oslo, 1953.

MACDONELL, A. A. and KEITH, A. B., *Vedic Index of Names and Subjects*, 2 vols, reprinted Delhi, 1958.

MACLEAN, UNA, *Magical Medicine*, Penguin, Harmondsworth, 1974.

MAIR, LUCY, *Witchcraft*, London, 1969; reprinted 1973.

MANI, V., *Puranic Encyclopaedia*, Delhi, 1975.
MÉTRAUX, A., *Voodoo*, André Deutsch, London, 1959.
MEYER, JOHN JACOB, *Trilogie altindischer Mächte und Feste der Vegetation*, 3 vols, Zurich and Leipzig, 1937.
MEYER, JOHN JACOB, *Sexual Life in Ancient India*, Eng. trans. Kegan Paul, London, 1952.
MICHAEL, HENRY N. (ed.), *Studies in Siberian Shamanism*, University of Toronto, 1963; reprinted 1972.
MOÏNFAR, M. (ed.), *Mélanges E. Benveniste*, Paris, 1975.
MOLÉ, M., *Culte, mythe et cosmologie dans l'Iran ancien*, Paris, 1963.
MUKHOPADYAYA, G., *The Surgical Instruments of the Hindus with a Comparative Study of the Surgical Instruments of Greek, Roman, Arab, and Modern European Surgeons*; reprinted 1977.
MÜLLER, R. F. G., 'Der Takman des Atharvaveda', *Artibus Asiae*, vol. 6, 1937.
NEWALL, VENETIA (ed.), *The Witch Figure*, Routledge & Kegan Paul, London, 1973.
NILSSON, M.P., *A History of Greek Religion*, trans. F. J. Fielden, Oxford University Press, 1925.
OBERMAN, J., *Ugaritic Mythology*, Yale University Press, 1948.
O'FLAHERTY, W., 'The Hindu symbolism of cows, bulls, stallions and mares' (*Art and Archaeology Research Papers*, No. 8), London, 1975.
OHANA, J., *La Chance*, Paris, 1948.
PADDAYYA, K., *Investigations into the Neolithic Culture of the Shorapur Doab, South India*, Leiden, 1973.
PEATE, I. C., *Tradition and Folk Life. A Welsh View*, Faber, 1972.
PETITPIERRE, DOM ROBERT (ed.), *Exorcism*, SPCK, London, 1975.
PIGGOTT, STUART, *Prehistoric India*, Penguin, Harmondsworth, 1950; reprinted 1962.
PIGGOTT, STUART (ed.), *The Dawn of Civilization*, Thames & Hudson, London, 1961.
PILLAI, G. S., *Tree Worship and Ophiolatry*, Trichinopoly, 1948.
POSENER, GEORGES (ed.), *A Dictionary of Egyptian Civilization*, Methuen, London, 1962.
PUHVEL, JAAN (ed.), *Myth and Law Among the Indo-Europeans*, University of California, 1970.
RADFORD, E. and RADFORD, M. A., *Encyclopaedia of Superstitions*, ed. and rev. by Christina Hole, 1961; reprinted 1969, Hutchinson.
RAWSON, J., *Animals in Art*, British Museum, 1977.
REINER, ERICA, *Šurpu. A Collection of Sumerian and Akkadian Incantations*, Osnabrück, 1970.
RENOU, L., *Les Écoles Védiques et la formation du Veda*, 1947.

RENOU, L., *Religions of Ancient India*, Athlone Press, London, 1953.
RIDGEWAY, WILLIAM, *The Origin and Influence of the Thoroughbred Horse*, Cambridge University Press, 1905.
RODINSON, MAXIME, *Mohammed*, Allen Lane, London, 1973.
ROHDE, ERWIN, *Deliver Us from Evil. Studies on the Vedic Ideas of Salvation*, Lund, 1946.
ROHDE, ERWIN, *Psyche*, trans. W. R. Hillis, Kegan Paul, London, 1925.
ROHEIM, GEZA, *Magic and Schizophrenia*, New York, 1955.
RUNEBERG, A., *Witches, Demons and Fertility Magic*, Helsinki, 1947.
SARGANT, W., *The Mind Possessed*, Heinemann, London, 1973.
SCOTT, C., *An Outline of Modern Occultism*, Dutton, New York; 2nd edn, 1950.
SHENDE, N. J., *The Religion and Philosophy of the Atharvaveda*, Poona, 1952.
SIGERIST, HENRY E., *A History of Medicine*, 2 vols, New York, Oxford University Press, 1961.
SINGH, S. D., *Ancient Indian Warfare with special references to the Vedic Period*, Leiden, 1965.
SOLOMON, ESTHER A., 'Skambha-hymns of the Atharva-veda', *Journal Oriental Instit., Baroda*, vol. 9, 1960, pp. 233ff.
SPIEGEL, F., *Die arische Periode und ihre Zustande*, Leipzig, 1887.
STEUER, R. O. *et al.*, *Ancient Egyptian and Cnidian Medicine*, California, 1959.
STONE, ERIC, *Medicine among the American Indians*, New York, 1932.
STUTLEY, M. and STUTLEY, J., *A Dictionary of Hinduism*, London, Routledge & Kegan Paul, 1977.
THOMPSON, R. C., *The Devils and Evil Spirits of Babylonia*, 2 vols, Luzac, London, 1903.
THOMPSON, R. C., *Semitic Magic*, Luzac, London, 1908.
THORWALD, JURGEN, *Science and Secrets of Early Medicine*, trans. by R. & C. Winston, Thames & Hudson, London, 1962.
TURNER, R. L., *A Comparative Dictionary of the Indo-Aryan Languages*, School of Oriental and African Studies, 1966.
UCKO, PETER J. and DIMBLEBY, G. W. (eds), *The Domestication and Exploitation of Plants and Animals*, Duckworth, London, 1969.
VAIHINGER, H., *The Philosophy of 'As If'*, trans. C. K. Ogden, Kegan Paul, London, 1935.
VIENNOT, ODETTE, *Le Culte de l'arbre dans l'Inde ancienne*, Paris, 1954.
WAKE, ARCHBISHOP, *et al.* (trans.), *The Forbidden Books of the Original New Testament of Jesus Christ*, T. Owen, London, 1878.
WASSON, R. GORDON, *Soma, Divine Mushroom of Immortality*, New

York/The Hague, 1969; reprinted 1971.

WASSON, R. GORDON, *Soma and the Fly-Agaric*, Botanical Museum of Harvard University, 1972.

WHITING, J. W. M., 'Sorcery, Sin and the Superego', in *Nebraska Symposium on Motivation*, ed. M. R. Jones, Nebraska, 1959.

WHITNEY, WILLIAM DWIGHT, *The Atharva-Veda Saṁhitā*, 2 vols, HOS, 1905; reprinted Delhi, 1962.

WHITNEY, WILLIAM DWIGHT, *The Century Dictionary*, 8 vols, New York, 1891; reprinted 1899.

WHITNEY, WILLIAM DWIGHT, *The Atharva-veda Prātiśākhya*, Varanasi, 1962.

WHITNEY, WILLIAM DWIGHT and ROTH, R., *Atharva Veda Saṁhitā*, Berlin, 1924.

WIER, JEAN, *Histoires, Disputes et Discours des Illusions et Impostures des Diables*, 1579.

WIKANDER, S., *Feuerpriester in Kleinasien und Iran*, Lund, 1946.

WINTERNITZ, M., *A History of Indian Literature*, vol. I, pt 1, trans. by Mrs S. Ketkar, Calcutta, 1959.

ZAEHNER, R. C., *Zurvan*, Oxford University Press, 1955.

ZAEHNER, R. C. (ed.), *The Concise Encyclopaedia of Living Faiths*, Boston, 1959.

ZIMMER, H. R., *Hindu Medicine*, Baltimore, 1948.

ZIMMER, H. R., *Myths and Symbols in Indian Art and Civilization*, ed. J. Campbell, New York, 1946; reprinted 1972.

Index

bows, 70–1
Brahmā, 52
Brāhmaṇa class, 79, 127
Brahmaṇaspati, 68, 124, 129
brahmaudana, 48, 54, 87, 123
brahmavidyā, 2
breath, 44–6; and birth, 55; and contraception, 50; triple exhalation, 55–6
Bṛhaddevatā, 3
Bṛhaspati: and battle, 77; concord, 129; cows, 85; herbs, 39; oblation to, 82; *purohita*, 62–3
Buddhism, 40; immortality, 41; saviour, 69
buildings, *see* house
bull hide, 64
burning, 94–5

cakra, 71
carts, and ritual, 24
caru, 57
Caspian horses, 72
cātanāni spells, 57, 92
Catholic rites, *see* Christian belief
cattle, *see* cows
cavalry, 72
Celtic legend: effigies, 99; festivals, 118; horses, 30; owls, 108; weapons, 71
chance, 115
chariots, war, 72, 73, 123
Christian belief: breath, 44–5, 46, 55–6; curses and blessings, 101; death, 86–7; expiation, 105; gold, 43; horses, 30; immortality, 48; Mass, and magic, 86–7, 90; psalms, dual purpose, 4, 93; rain, prayers for, 121–2; saliva, 32; saviour, 69; and witchcraft, 88
church, sleeping in, 21
circles, symbolism, 46–7
class, social, 79–80, 127
clay effigies, 99
cocks, night-crowing, 82
colic, remedies for, 37–8
Coll (island): remedies, 23
colour: of skin, 51, 57, 79, 127; of witchcraft, 15, 77
communal land, division, 116–17
community: and harmony, 127–8; influence in, 129–30, 131
complexion: colour, 51, 57, 79, 127; of sons, 57
conception, 54–5
concord, *see* harmony
confession, 105
confluence of rivers, 17, 33
constipation, 16–17
consumption, *see* tuberculosis
contraception, *see* birth control
Cornwall, holed stones, 23
Corp Creadh, 99
cows: barren, 82–3, 84–5, 113; charms for, 117–19; donation to priest, 81–6; dung, 114, 117, 122; and expiation, 106; at funeral rites, 83–4; importance, 114, 117; killing, 86; and luck, 108; products, 106, 114, 117; punching, 83, 118–19; red, 84; stolen, 85–6, 114; twin, 117; urine, 34–5; and victory rites, 77; as wealth, 114; and witchcraft, 84, 86
creation, 49–50, 127
Crick (Creeping) Stone, 23
crops, division of, 116–17
crossroads, 38, 123–4
curses, 92–3, 101–2; personification, 101; repealing, 96, 101–2
Cyavana, 128–9

Dākṣāyaṇas, 43
Dakṣiṇā, 50, 80–2, 110
dance, war, 72
danger, 88
darbha grass, 38, 39, 69, 77, 131

Isaac, 82, 101

Jacob, 101, 115
jālāṣa, 34
Jamadagni, 32
Jāmi, 52
Jara, 43
jaundice: cures, 19–20; salves, 31
jāyānya, 35–6
jealousy, 59
Jinns, 93
jvara, 11, 12

Kālakāñjas, 37
Kalkin, 69
Kāma, 53
kapitthaka tree, 26
Kapota, 107
Kauśika Sūtra, 2–3
khadira wood, 117
Khvarənah, 67
kings, 61–9; aspiring, 64–5; attributes of, 61, 62, 64, 66–7, 67–8; in battle, 73–4; consecration of, 63–5, 123; divine status of, 61–2, 67; and elephants, 66, 67; functions of, 64; and penance, 106; and priests, 86; and protection, 65, 66; and *purohitas*, 62–6; restoration of, 68–9, 73; support of, 62; and tiger-skins, 64
knots, untying, 57
Kṛtyā, 15, 77, 96–8
Kṣatra class, 127
Kṣetrapati, 120
Kṣetriya, cures, 22–4
Kuśika, 100
kuṣṭha plant, 13–14, 31, 52, 53

Lakṣmī, 115
laying-on of hands, 9
lead amulets, 91–2
left (inauspicious) side, 51, 55, 98
lelo, 40
leprosy, cures for, 22
livestock, 117
living standards, 122
lockjaw, 47
longevity, charms for, 41–8, 67
Lord's Prayer, 90
lost objects, recovery of, 123–4
love: charms for, 52–4; fragrant spells and potions, 53, 54; gaining, 52–5; in literature, 60
luck: in gambling, 122–3; and women, 60
lumbago, cures for, 23

magic, *see* witchcraft
Manasā, 30–1
mantras, 2; atharvavedic, 3; against enemies, 99–100; battle, 73; inverted, 90; for longevity, 41, 45; love, 52–3; in medicine, 8–9; and omens, 107; powerful, 100; purifying, 112; and stolen cows, 85–6; thwarting, 94; and witchcraft, 90
Manu, Code of, 87
manure, *see* excrement
Manyu, 78, 130
marmāṇi, 98
marriage, 51–2, 54, 60
Maruts, 121
Masai tribe, 83
mascots, 117
Mass, and black magic, 86–7, 90
mātṛnāmāni charms, 38
medicine: charms, 7–40; excremental, 34; and the mind, 40; origins, 6, 7–9, 20; plants, healing, 11, 36–7; substances, 8
Mên-an-Tol stone, 23
Métraux, A., 97
Mexico, ancient: gold in, 43
mice, removal of, 120
migraine, cure for, 20
Milky Way: name for, 84
miscarriage, prevention of, 57–8

Mithra, 43–4
Mitra, 43–4, 82, 121, 126
Mohammed, 76
mohanāni, 70
moles: and agriculture, 120; and constipation, 16
Monier-Williams, M., 16, 84
moon: and harmony, 126; and plants, 11
Moses, 18, 93
mṛgārāṇi charms, 124
Mṛtyu, 41, 63, 77
Mūjavant, 14
muñja grass, 57, 110
murder, expiation of, 110–11
musical instruments, in war, 71–2
mustard, 58
muttering, 41, 68, 105

Naciketas, 81
naghāmāra, 14
naghāriṣa, 14
Nairṛta, 107
names, importance of, 14, 31, 94, 105
Namuci, 92
Nārada, 84, 85
nationalism, 127
nature, and harmony, 126
Nesi-Amsu papyrus, 98
neuralgia, 37–8
Nias Islands, disease-transference in, 20–1
nightmares, 81; and expiation, 104, 109
Nirṛti, 45; colour, 58, 111–12; and doves, 107; goddess of destruction, 41, 44, 47, 91, 103, 107, 113, 127; and misfortune, 2; offerings to, 98; and quarrels, 127; and witchcraft, 111–12
Nitatnī, 32–3
numbers, significance of, 34, 110
Nyarbudi, 76

obesity, remedies for, 39
objects, passing between, 24
oblations, 82; and battle, 73, 75; by kings, 67, 73; and prosperity, 115, 122; and sorcerers, 91
odana, see brahmaudana
ointments, 31
omens: bad, 82, 107–9, 111, 117; and war, 73
Oṣadhipati, 11
owls, 108–9

Paidva, 29, 30
Paippalada priestly school, 3
pairings, 33, 82, 115
Palestine: houses in, 115
Pandarus, 18
paralysis, remedies for, 28, 37
parivyādha plant, 27
Parjanya, 16, 121, 124
parturition, easy, 56
Pāṭā plant, 130
peace, 131; *see also* harmony
pearl-shell amulets, 31, 43
pebbles, twenty-one, 75–6, 123–4
Pedu, 29
penances, 36, 105–6
peppercorns, personified, 38
perfume, *see* fragrant charms
personification, 12
pests, removal of, 120
phantoms: charms against, 99; conjuring, 76
Pharaohs, 64, 66
phaṭ, 52–3
Philadelphia University Museum, 7
philtres, 8
pigeons, 108
Piṅga, 56
Piśācas, 45, 95
planets: and disease, 10; importance of, 126
plants: curse-effacing, 93; dark, 22; fragrant, 53, 54; healing, 4,

11, 36–7; to escape penalties, 39–40; rough, 59; against witchcraft, 95–6
ploughs, 119; and expiation, 112; personification of, 119; in ritual, 23–4
poetry, women in, 60
poison, remedies for, 26, 27–30
political power, 129–30
portents, inauspicious, 31; *see also* omens
power, 129–30
Prajāpati, 37, 44, 50, 73, 78, 97, 121, 124, 131
prayer, power of, 77
precedence, inversion of, 109–10
pregnancy, 55–8
priests: attacks on, 86–7; and charms, 79–87; cows, donation to, 81–6, 119; and enemies, 86–7; families of, 1; and fire, 3–4, 42; income of, 80–2; power of, 79, 80; protection of, 79
prosperity: agricultural, 114–15, 116–22; charms for, 114–25; political, 129–30; sharing, 116–17; and trade, 122
protection, 102
Psalms and cursing, 4, 93
puṁsavana rite, 55–6
punching of cattle, 83, 118–19
punishment, 94–5
purification: and *apāmārga*, 112; and cows, 106; by water, 13, 24, 33–4, 41, 51, 64; and longevity, 41
Purohita: in battle, 72, 77; function of, 5, 62–6, 80; prestige of, 63
puruṣa sūkta, 127
Pūṣan, 56, 109, 123, 124, 129
pūtudru wood amulet, 44–5

quarrels, 127–9

rājanya class, 79, 127
rājasūya rite, 63–4, 65, 68
rākṣasas, 45, 91
rāṣṭrabhṛts, 73
Rātrī, 109
red, symbolism, 15, 19, 77
reeds, burning, 95
religion, neglect of, 113
reparation, 104
reversal and magic, 90
Ṛgveda, 1–2, 3; and agriculture, 119; and marriage, 51; and medicine, 7; and pre-Aryan times, 70; and witchcraft, 89
Ṛgvidhāna, 3, 41, 64–5, 68, 75, 89, 118
Rhea, 18
rheumatism: charms against, 17–18; ointments for, 31
rice, symbolism, 58
Ridgeway, W., 72
rites, dual purpose, 4; errors in, 111, 112
rivals, eliminating, 49, 58–60, 89–90, 95
rivers, confluence of, 17, 33
rod, symbolism, 18
Roman Catholic rites, *see* Christian belief
Romans: and owls, 108
royalty: and charms, 61–9; consecration of, 63–5; *see also* kings
Rudra, 12, 14, 34, 37, 77, 78, 83, 85, 124
rulers, *see* kings

sabhā, 131
Śacī, 67
sacrifice: blood, 110–11; enemy's, 102–3; errors, 111, 112; fees, 80; between feet, 116; and women, 50
sadānvās, 57, 95
Śakadruma, 122
saliva, symbolism, 32, 35
salves, 31, 43

tears, of priests, 87
teeth: danger of, 113; pain in, 24–5
tiger-skin, symbolism, 64
Timor-haut: epilepsy in, 21
toothache, 24–5
trade and prosperity, 122
trance, 122
transference of disease, 17, 18, 19
transgressions: expiation of, 104–13; relief from penalty for, 39–40
Triṇāman, 129
Triśiras, 12
Trita, 40, 109, 110
tuberculosis, 26; cures for, 21, 23
Tvaṣṭṛ, 60, 68, 110, 124
twelve, significance of, 110
twins, 82, 104, 117

ucchuṣmā plant, 26–7
'Unfasteners', 23, 24
Upaniṣads, 2; and creation, 49–50; and immortality, 48; and witchcraft, 89–90
urination, expiation of, 113
urine, as remedy, 34–5, 106
Uzziah, King, 22

vadhaka wood, 74
Vaikhānasas, 89
vaiśya class, 79, 127
Vaitahavya family, 85
Vaitaraṇī river, 84
Vājapeya ceremony, 65
vajra, 71, 74
Varaṇāvatī, 28
varaṇa wood, 39
Varuṇa: bonds of, 36; and dropsy, 10, 33; and law and order, 126, 129; oblation to, 82; and snake venom, 28; and Soma, 84; and sovereignty, 63; and virility, 26; and water, 10, 120–1
Vasiṣṭha(s), 63, 99–100, 121
Vāstoṣpati, 116, 129
Vasus, 129
Vedas, 2, 81
Vedic Age, 1; cows, 83, 114; horses, 72; houses, 115–16; kings, 69; longevity, 41; medicine, 78; nature and harmony, 126; priests, 4; trade, 122; witchcraft, 89; women, 49
vibhītaka wood, 90
victory rites, 77
vihavya prayer, 103
Viliptī, 84–5
village assembly, 131
Virgin Mary, 99
virility, restoration of, *see* impotence
Viṣṇu, 13, 69, 71, 94
Viśvāmitra, 42, 63, 100
Viśvarūpa, 85, 110
Viśvedevas, 82
Voodoo, 96, 97–8, 100
Vṛtra, 94
vulnerability, 98

wailing, 47–8
Wales: birth customs, 56; black animals, 107; disease remedies, 21, 35; omens, 108; owls, 108; pigeons, 108
Wanga, 97–8
war, *see* battle
Wasson, R. G., 74
water, 33; and agriculture, 120–2; bathing the dead, 87; and fever, 12–13; and pain, 33–4; and purification, 13, 24, 33–4, 41, 51, 64; and wounds, 22
wax effigies, 98–9
wealth, *see* prosperity
weapons, 70–1, 75–6, 77–8; personification, 71
weather forecasting, 122
wedding ceremonies, 56
wheel, symbolism, 68